RURAL TOURISM

RURAL TOURISM

By

Charlie Sampson

DISCOVERY PUBLISHING HOUSE PVT. LTD.

NEW DELHI-110 002

First Published - 2011

Reprinted - 2016

ISBN: 978-81-8356-944-6

Rural Tourism

Published by:

DISCOVERY PUBLISHING HOUSE PVT. LTD.

4383/4B, Ansari Road, Darya Ganj
New Delhi-110 002 (India)
Phone: +91-11-23279245, 43596064-65
Fax: +91-11-23253475
E-mail: discoverypublishinghouse@gmail.com
sales@discoverypublishinggroup.com
web: www.discoverypublishinggroup.com

Printed at:
Infinity Imaging Systems
Delhi

PREFACE

It is an ideal and natural method of rural and urban economic exchange. Rural tourism is particularly relevant in developing nations wherein farmland has become fragmented due to population growth. Rural tourism exists in developed nations in the form of providing accommodation in a scenic location ideal for rest and relaxation. It is a mixture of many tourism like farm or agricultural tourism, cultural tourism, nature tourism and adventure tourism. It also covers eco-tourism a little bit.

Rural tourism allows the creation of an alternative source of income in the non-agricultural sector for rural dwellers. The added income from rural tourism can contribute to the revival of lost folk art and handicrafts. Many niche tourism programs are located in rural areas. From wine tours and eco-tourism, to agritourism and seasonal events, tourism can be a viable economic component in rural community development. According the USDA, Cooperative State, Education and Extension Service, "Tourism is becoming increasingly important to the U.S. economy.

Folk culture refers to the lifestyle of a culture. Historically, handed down through oral tradition, it demonstrates the "old ways" over novelty and relates to a sense of community. Folk culture is quite often imbued with a sense of place. If elements of a folk culture are copied by, or moved to, a foreign locale, they will still carry strong connotations of their original place of creation. Rural tourism related activities have been widely regarded as key-tools for rural development, especially in those countries where rural areas are in abundance as Romania and all East European countries where rural space and production is still a major part of whole economic structure, trying by this way to revitalize declining areas and ensure them possibilities of achieving a sustainable future.

Tourism is the second largest foreign exchange earner in Morocco, after the phosphate industry.The Moroccan government is heavily investing in tourism development. A new tourism strategy called Vision 2010 was developed after the accession of King Mohammed VI in 1999. The government has targeted that Morocco will have 10 million visitors by 2010, with the hope that tourism will then have risen to 20% of GDP. A large government sponsored marketing campaigns to attract tourists advertised Morocco as a cheap and exotic, yet safe, place for European tourists.

While compiling research material for this book, we search many websites, visit many libraries for ensuring the authenticity of the matter and current updates. We are sincerely grateful to all these resources as without this the publication of this book wouldn't have been possible. Our main aim is to spread the light of knowledge to the readers, so that the darkness of ignorance dispels away.

—Author

CONTENTS

1 Introduction to Rural Tourism

If you are thinking of fresh air flowing in natural surroundings amidst cuckoo singing with full throat, then go for rural tourism. Rural tourism is a tourist activity which takes place far from the maddening crowd of city. It is a mixture of many tourism like farm or agricultural tourism, cultural tourism, nature tourism and adventure tourism. It also covers eco-tourism a little bit.

It focuses on participating in a rural lifestyle, where life is slow but beautiful. A typical type of tourism that showcases the rural lifestyle accentuated with art, culture and heritage at rural locations, thereby benefiting the local community economically and socially as well as enabling interaction between the tourists and the locals for a more enriching tourism experience can be termed as rural tourism. Rural tourism has certain typical traits like it is innovative, the locations are sparsely populated, it is predominantly in natural landscape, it meshes with seasonality and local events and is based on preservation of culture, heritage and traditions.

It can be a variant of ecotourism. Any village can be a tourist attraction, and many villagers are very hospitable. Agriculture is becoming highly mechanized and therefore requires less manual labor. This is causing economic pressure on some villages, leading to an exodus of young people to urban areas.

It is an ideal and natural method of rural and urban economic exchange. Rural tourism is particularly relevant in developing nations wherein farmland has become fragmented due to population growth. Rural tourism exists in developed nations in the form of providing accommodation in a scenic location ideal for rest and relaxation.

There have been cows on Colemans Farm for last four centuries, but these days they're just for show. Even on a drenched autumn day, the farm is one of the Isle of Wight's perkier tourist attractions: flocks of squealing schoolchildren make friends with bleating goats and clucking chickens.

When Neil and Karen Dickson bought Colemans in 1999, it was a working farm. But it had a licence to open to the public, and the island location persuaded the Dicksons that it could make more money farming tourists.

And so it proved. On their first day, the Dicksons had 600 visitors; last year, they had 60,000, and growth rates have been 30-40% annually. The farm is now profitable, and the Dicksons are planning a big expansion next year.

"We seem to have hit on something basic that children really love," says Mrs Dickson.

The foot-and-mouth outbreak of 2001 seemed a catastrophe for the business. Across the UK, 80% of country parks, 90% of farms and more than one-third of historic properties were closed to visitors. And the trade won none of the lavish post-epidemic compensation that went to farmers.

Since then, however, the recovery has been far brisker than anyone predicted.

"In a way, foot-and-mouth was good news," says Nigel Embry, chief executive of Farm Stay UK, a network of 1,100 agri-tourism businesses. "It created awareness about what the countryside has to offer."

Now, tourism supports 380,000 jobs in rural areas, more than making up for a decline of more than 150,000 in the agricultural workforce. Overall, its contribution to rural economic output is reckoned to be almost £14bn.

RURAL AREA

Rural areas are large and isolated areas of an open country with low population density. The terms "countryside" and "rural areas" are not synonyms, the former refers to rural areas that are open. Forest, wetlands, and other areas with a low population density are not countryside.

About 91 percent of the rural population now earn salaried incomes, often in urban areas. The 10 percent who still produce resources generate 20 percent of the world's coal, copper, and oil; 10 percent of its wheat, 20 percent of its meat, and 50 percent of its corn. The efficiency of these farms is due in large part to the commercialization of the farming industry, and not single family operations.

United States

Approximately 80 percent United States' inhabitants live in suburban and urban areas, but cities occupy only 10 percent of the country. Rural areas occupy the remaining 90 percent. The U.S. Census Bureau, the USDA's Economic Research Service, and the Office of Management and Budget (OMB) have come together to help define rural areas. The Census Bureau definitions (new to the 2000 census), which are based on population density, defines rural areas as all territory outside of Census Bureau-defined urbanized areas and urban clusters. An urbanized area consists of a central city and surrounding areas whose population ("urban nucleus") is greater than 50,000.

They may or may not contain individual cities with 50,000 or more; rather, they must have a core with a population density generally exceeding 1,000 persons per square mile; and may contain adjoining territory with at least 500 persons per square mile (other towns outside of an urbanized area whose population exceeds 2,500). Thus, rural areas comprise open country and settlements with fewer than 2,500 residents; areas designated as rural can have population densities as high as 999 per square mile or as low as 1 person per square mile.

The USDA's Office of Rural Development may define rural by various population thresholds. The 2002 farm bill defined rural and rural area as any area other than (a) a city or town that has a population of greater than 50,000 inhabitants, and (b) the urbanized areas contiguous and adjacent to such a city or town. The rural-urban continuum codes, urban influence codes, and rural county typology codes developed by USDA's Economic Research Service (ERS) allow researchers to break out the standard metropolitan and nonmetropolitan areas into smaller residential groups.

For example, a metropolitan county is one that contains an urbanized area, or one that has a twenty-five percent commuter rate to an urbanized area regardless of population.;OMB: Under the Core Based Statistical Areas used by the OMB, a metropolitan county, or Metropolitan Statistical Area, consists of (a) central counties with one or more urbanized areas (as defined by the Census Bureau) and (b) outlying counties that are economically tied to the core counties as measured by worker commuting data (i.e. if 25% of workers living there commute to the core counties, or if 25% of the employment in the county consists of workers coming from the central counties). Non-metro counties are outside the boundaries of metro areas and are further subdivided into Micropolitan Statistical Areas centered on urban clusters of 10,000-50,000 residents, and all remaining non-core counties.

Rural Schools

National Center for Education Statistics (NCES) revised its definition of rural schools in 2006 after working with the Census Bureau to create a new locale classification system to capitalize on improved geocoding technology and the 2000 Office of Management and Budget (OMB) definitions of metro areas that rely less on population size and county boundaries than proximity of an address to an urbanized area. The new classification system has four major local categories— city, suburban, town, and rural —each of which is subdivided into three subcategories.

Cities and suburbs are subdivided into the categories small, midsize, or large; towns and rural areas are subdivided by their proximity to an urbanized area into the categories fringe, distant, or remote. These twelve categories are based on several key concepts that Census uses to define an area's urbanicity: principal city, urbanized area, and urban cluster. Rural areas are designated by census as those areas that do not lie inside an urbanized area or urban cluster.

NCES has classified all schools into one of these twelve categories based on schools' actual addresses and their corresponding coordinates of latitude and longitude. Not only does this mean that the location of any school can be identified precisely, but also that distance measures can be used to identify town and rural subtypes."

Rural Health

Rural health definitions can be different for establishing underserved areas or health care accessibility in rural areas of the United States. According to the handbook, Definitions of Rural: A Handbook for Health Policy Makers and Researchers, "Residents of metropolitan counties are generally thought to have easy access to the relatively concentrated health services of the county's central areas. However, some metropolitan counties are so large that they contain small towns and rural, sparsely populated areas that are isolated from these central clusters and their corresponding health services by physical barriers." To address this type of rural area, "Harold Goldsmith, Dena Puskin, and Dianne Stiles (1992) described a methodology to identify small towns and rural areas within large metropolitan counties (LMCs) that were isolated from central areas by distance or other physical features." This became the Goldsmith Modification definition of rural. "The Goldsmith Modification has been useful for expanding the eligibility for federal programs that assist rural populations—to include the isolated rural populations of large metropolitan counties."

UNITED KINGDOM

In Britain, "rural" is defined by the government Department for Environment, Food and Rural Affairs (DEFRA), using population data from the latest census, such as the United Kingdom Census 2001. These definitions have various grades, but the upper point is any local government area with less than 26% of its population living in a market town ("market town" being defined as any settlement which has permission to hold a street market).

Rural Health

An NHS patient is defined as rural if they live more than 5 km from either a doctor or a dispensing chemist. This is important for defining whether the patient is expected to collect their own medicines. While doctors' surgeries in towns will not have a dispensing chemist, instead expecting patients to use a high-street chemist to purchase their prescription medicines, in rural village surgeries, an NHS dispensary will be built into the same building.

Eco-friendly Rural Tourism

In its endeavor to promote the livelihood opportunities of the rural people in the state, NABARD has sanctioned environment friendly rural tourism project in three villages, namely, Hong, Siibey and Biiri in Ziro area of Lower Subansiri district.

The project was sanctioned to Young Mission Adventure Club (YMAC), a local NGO-based in Itanagar which has been actively engaged in tourism related activities with the support of NABARD and other agencies.

Recently, NABARD deputed Y. Yomngam, Secretary of the YMAC for "On Location Training on Village Tourism" in Sikkim, where the scheme has been successfully implemented for income and employment generation during the past few years.

The objective of the proposal is to develop a replicable rural tourism model in Ziro area through -Capacity building Village of community to cater to tourists in Home Stays, promotion of villages as eco-tourists /village tourist destination , develop villages as Community based Tourist Spot, increasing socio-economic status of rural people through Eco/village tourism, increase community participation level and to develop sense of ownership and belongingness, conservation of biodiversity, environment, culture and tradition, generation of self employment for educated unemployed youth, drop-outs, house-wives,SHGs etc.

The project is to be implemented within a period of one year with different activities spreading over the project period. Successful implementation of the project is expected to result in rise in awareness level on rural tourism, rise in the number of people undertaking Rural Tourism activities, income level, employment generation, better waste management, better protection to environment and women etc.

The Deputy Commissioner, Lower Subansiri has issued Letter of Comfort for implementation of the project. District Level Tourism Monitoring Committee would be guiding and monitoring the successful implementation of the project.

With the collective efforts and involvement of various stakeholders, the venture is expected to give boost to development of viable and replicable model for growth of rural tourism in the state, according to an official release.

Pins and Needles

The lure of easy money is strong. But Nick Evans, who runs the Centre for Rural Research at University College Worcester, warns that tourism is no panacea for every cash-strapped farmer.

For a start, he says, the realistic profit to be made from a tourism sideline is little better than pin-money. "Self-catering accommodation ventures are the ones that most farmers want to diversify into," he says.

Unfortunately, this is also the form of diversification venture that most frequently fails to be successful. Farms with grander ambitions often get parcelled up in red tape: B&Bs aiming to accommodate more,than six guests, for example, are required to comply wth demanding fire regulations; farmers offering land for more than five caravans have to seek a licence from the local authority.

"Setting up a tourism venture can require a large initial capital investment - money that struggling farm businesses simply do not have," he says.

If expectations of income are low, tourism can be run as a complementary sideline. Farms tend to have plentiful barely-used space, ripe for conversion; a B&B or holiday cottage can be run by a less busy family member.

A full makeover like Colemans Farm demands effort, but taking in the odd guest need not disrupt the settled habits of farming life: farm-stay visitors actively want a whiff of manure.

And tourism may be vaguely seasonal, but often in ways that suit a farmer's schedule: the peak for many tourist businesses would be in high summer, before the demands of the harvest kick in.

The government is certainly convinced. As part of a package of measures after the foot-and-mouth outbreak, it has shifted responsibility for rural tourism onto the Regional Development Agencies. These RDAs, which have previously tended to focus more on urban needs, will be obliged to think of ways to fit tourism into broader rural regeneration plans, including investment in everything from education to transport.

Agency, which helps coordinate rural affairs for the government, warns that tourism may be getting more attention than its success merits.

"Tourism is very high profile, but that's not the same as being regenerative," he says.

"Sectors like health or retailing account for the vast majority of jobs in the countryside, but the policy emphasis is still on traditional industries such as farming and tourism. It seems strange."

Despite its growth, tourism makes up just nine percent of rural employment; manufacturing, meanwhile, employs one in four rural workers, and is growing at a fair clip. Policy, then, could be being influenced by a sentimental and unrealistic view of the rural economy. The truth is uglier - but possibly far more prosperous.

Rural tourism allows the creation of an alternative source of income in the non-agricultural sector for rural dwellers. The added income from rural tourism can contribute to the revival of lost folk art and handicrafts.

Non-agricultural rural employment accounts for an increasing proportion of total rural employment in Latin America. Its potential for stimulating rural development has been noted, but it has also been analysed as a focal point of poverty. It is noted that non-agricultural rural employment is heterogeneous and different types of employment arise in response to different dynamics. Although, there are potential sources of non-agricultural rural employment which have no connection with agriculture, in the countries analysed it is the characteristics of the agricultural sector which influence most heavily the composition and characteristics of such employment.

Agriculture influences both the generation of non-agricultural productive employment and the creation of makeshift alternative jobs, primarily through demand for non-agricultural goods and services and the discharge of surplus labour. Consequently, in order for non-agricultural rural activities to make a significant contribution to rural development it is necessary to adopt an approach which integrates both the agricultural and non-agricultural elements of such development

Rural Areas in United States

Many niche tourism programs are located in rural areas. From wine tours and eco-tourism, to agritourism and seasonal events, tourism can be a viable economic component in rural community development. According the USDA, Cooperative State, Education and Extension Service, "Tourism is becoming increasingly important to the U.S. economy.

A conservative estimate from the Federal Reserve Board in Kansas, based on 2000 data, shows that basic travel and tourism industries accounted for 3.6 percent of all U.S. employment. Even more telling, data from the Travel Industry Association of America indicate that one out of every 18 people in the U.S. has a job directly resulting from travel expenditures."

Folk Culture

It refers to the lifestyle of a culture. Historically, handed down through oral tradition, it demonstrates the "old ways" over novelty and relates to a sense of community. Folk culture is quite often imbued with a sense of place. If elements of a folk culture are copied by, or moved to, a foreign locale, they will still carry strong connotations of their original place of creation.

Examples of American folk cultures include:

- Powwows
- Native tribal regalia
- The cakewalk
- Louisiana Creole cuisine, music, and language
- Handmade quilts
- The Hawaiian hula, leis, a pantheon of nature gods, and the concept of aloha
- Shaker architecture and furniture
- Whale-hunting with traditional spiritual rites of some Alaskan tribes
- Tepees
- Hand-gathered Wild rice gleaned in the traditional manner in the United States' northwoods

The above-mentioned have entered mainstream consciousness to varying degrees, but none have been so distorted from their original form as to have lost their culturally specific sense of place. In contrast, blue jeans and McDonald's are cultural icons which have been made so internationalized they have lost their original sense of place, and they are no longer part of folk culture. Similarly, Federalist architecture was created in the United States, but in a style influenced by, and meant to appeal to, outside interests.

Folk culture has always informed pop culture and even high culture. The minuet dance of European court society was based on the dance of peasants. More recently, the archetypal costume of the cowboy has been reinvented in gleaming silver by disco dancers and strippers, and the consciously hubristic culture of the Amish has been portrayed for comic value in Hollywood films and reality shows.It is the emphasis on looking inward without reference to the outside that separates folk culture from pop culture.

Pow-wow: Gathering of Native People

A pow-wow is a gathering of North America's Native people. A modern pow-wow is a specific type of event where both Native American and non-Native American people meet to dance, sing, socialize, and honor American Indian culture. There is generally a dancing competition, often with significant prize money awarded. Pow-wows vary in length from one day session of 5 to 6 hours to three days. Major pow-wows or pow-wows called for a special occasion can be up to one week long.

The term also has been used to describe any gathering of Native Americans of any tribe, and as such is occasionally heard in older Western movies. The word has also been used to refer to a meeting, especially a meeting of powerful people such as officers in the military. However, such use can also be viewed as disrespectful to Native culture.

Planning for a pow-wow generally begins months, perhaps even a year, in advance of the event by a group of people usually referred to as a pow-wow committee. Pow wows may be sponsored by a tribal organization, by an American Native community within an urban area, a Native American Studies program or American Native club on a college or university campus, tribe, or any other organization that can provide startup funds, insurance, and volunteer workers.

A pow-wow committee consists of a number of individuals who do all the planning prior to the event. If a pow-wow has a sponsor, such as a tribe, college, or organization, many or all members of the committee may come from that group. The committee is responsible to recruit and hire the head staff, publicize the pow-wow, secure a location, and recruit vendors who pay for the right to set up and sell food or merchandise at the pow-wow.

The head staff of a pow-wow are generally hired by the pow-wow committee several months in advance, as the quality of the head staff can have an impact on attendance. To be chosen as part of the head staff is an honor, showing respect for the person's skills or dedication.

Arena Director

The arena director is the person in charge during the pow-wow. Sometimes the arena director is referred to as the whip man, sometimes the whip man is the arena director's assistant, and many pow-wows don't have a whip man. The arena director makes sure dancers are dancing during the pow-wow and that the drum groups know what type of song to sing. If there are contests the arena director is ultimately responsible for providing judges, though he often has another assistant who is the head judge. The arena director is also responsible for organizing any ceremonies that may be required during the pow-wow, such as when an eagle feather is dropped, and others as required. One of the main duties of the arena director is to ensure that the dance arena is treated with the proper respect from visitors to the pow wow.

Master of Ceremonies

The master of ceremonies, or MC, is the voice of the pow-wow. It is his job to keep the singers, dancers, and general public informed as to what is happening. The MC sets the schedule of events, and maintains the drum rotation, or order of when each drum group gets to sing. The MC is also responsible for filling any dead air time that may occur during the pow-wow, often with jokes. The MC often runs any raffles or other contests that may happen during the pow-wow.

Head Dancers

The head dancers consist of the Head Man Dancer and the Head Woman Dancer, and often Head Teen Dancers, Head Little Boy and Girl Dancers, Head Golden Age Dancers, and a Head Gourd Dancer if the pow-wow has a Gourd Dance. The head dancers lead the other dancers in the grand entry or parade of dancers that opens a pow-wow. In many cases, the head dancers are also responsible for leading the dancers during songs, and often dancers will not enter the arena unless the head dancers are already out dancing.

Music and Drum

Music for pow-wow dance competition and other activities is provided by a "Drum," a group of performers who play a large, specially designed drum and sing traditional songs. The number of members of a drum group may vary, but is usually at least four people, and can be far more. Some members of the drum group may wear traditional regalia and dance as well as drum, other times drummers simply wear street clothing. Drums usually rotate the duty of providing songs for the dancers, each taking a turn at the direction of the pow-wow management.

The Host Drum of the pow-wow is a drum group primarily responsible for providing music for the dancers to dance to. At an Intertribal pow-wow, two or more drums are hired to be the host drums. In some places there is a Host Northern Drum and a Host Southern Drum. Depending on the size of the pow-wow and the region where it is held, there may be many drums, representing nearly every tribe or community attending the pow-wow. At some pow-wows, the drums are judged on the quality of their performances, with prize money awarded to the winners.

Each drum has a Lead Singer who runs his or her drum and leads the singers while singing. Host drums are responsible for singing the songs at the beginning and end of a pow-wow session, generally a starting song, the grand entry song, a flag song, and a veterans or victory song to start the pow-wow, and a flag song, retreat song and closing song to end the pow-wow. Additionally, if a pow-wow has gourd dancing, the Southern Host Drum is often the drum that sings all the gourd songs, though another drum can perform them. The host drums are often called upon to sing special songs during the pow-wow.

A pow-wow is often set up as a series of large circles. The center circle is the dance arena, outside of which is a larger circle consisting of the MC's table, drum groups, and sitting areas for dancers and their families. Beyond these two circles for participants is an area for spectators, while outside of all are designated areas with vendor's booths, where one can buy food (including frybread and Indian tacos), music, jewelry, souvenirs, arts and crafts, beadwork, leather, and regalia supplies.

At outdoor pow-wows, this circle is often covered by either a committee-built arbor or tent, or each group, particularly the MC and the drums, will provide their own. While most of the time, a tent provides shelter from the sun, rain can also plague outdoor events. It is particularly important to protect the drums used by the drum groups, as they are sensitive to temperature changes and, if it rains, they cannot get wet. Most vendors provide their own tents or shelters at an outdoor pow-wow.

A pow-wow session begins with the Grand Entry and, in most cases, a prayer. The Eagle Staff leads the Grand Entry, followed by flags, then the dancers, while one of the host drums sings an opening song. This event is sacred in nature, some pow-wows do not allow filming or photography during this time, though others allow it.

If military veterans or active duty soldiers are present, they often carry the flags and eagle staffs. They are followed by the head dancers, then the remaining dancers usually enter the arena in a specific order: Men's Traditional, Men's Grass Dance, Men's Fancy, Women's Traditional, Women's Jingle, and Women's Fancy. Teens and small children then follow in the same order. Following the Grand Entry, the MC will invite a respected member of the community to give an invocation. The host drum that did not sing the Grand Entry song will then sing a Flag Song, followed by a Victory or Veterans' Song, during which the flags and staffs are posted at the MC's table.

Dances

Most of the various types of dances performed at a pow-wow are descended from the dances of the Plains tribes of Canada and the United States. Besides those for the opening and closing of a pow-wow session, the most common is the intertribal, where a drum will sing a song and anyone who wants to can come and dance. Similar dances are the round dance; crow hop when performed by a northern drum or a horse stealing song by a southern drum; there is also "double beat", "sneakup" and, for Women's Traditional and Jingle, "sidestep". Each of these songs have a different step to be used during them, but are open for dancers of any style.

Normal intertribal dancing is an individual activity, but there are also couples and group dances. Couples dances include the two step and owl dance. In a two step each couple follows the lead of the head dancers, forming a line behind them, whereas in an owl dance each couple dances alone. Group dances include the Snake and Buffalo dance, where the group dances to mimic the motions of a snake in the beginning of the dance, then change to mimic the actions of a herd of buffalo.

At pow-wows where there is a large Southern Plains community in the area, the Gourd Dance is often included before the start of the pow-wow sessions. The gourd dance originated with the Kiowa tribe, whence it spread, and is a society dance for veterans and their families. Unlike other dances, the gourd dance is normally performed with the drum in the center of the dance arena, not on the side.

Music

Pow-wow music is the American Indian drumming, singing, and dancing performed at pow-wows. Though there are many genres unique to different tribes pow-wow music is characterized by pan or intertribalism with the Plains cultures, the originators of the modern pow-wow, predominating. For information on dancing, see #Dances.

Drumming

"Good drums get the dancers out there, good songs get them to dance well. Without drum groups there is no music. No music, no dance, no powwow."

There may be many drums at a powwow, especially weekend or week long ones, but each powwow features a host drum which is accorded great respect and the most authority. The members of drum groups are often family, extended family, or friends. Groups are then often named for families, geographic locations, tribal societies, or more colorful names. Many groups display their names on jackets, caps, vehicles, and chairs.

Traditionally only men would drum and women would sit behind the men singing high harmonies. Beginning in the mid 1970s, women began drumming with men and seconding, or singing, an octave higher, the song. Today, there are mixed-gender and all-female drum groups.

The supplies a drum group carries include the drum, rawhide headed, a cloth bag for padded drum sticks, the drum stand, folding chairs for sitting, and, in some cases, a public address system. The drum head, stand, microphone stands, and PA box are often decorated with paintings or eagle feathers, fur, flags, and strips of colored cloth.

Readily noticeable in performances are the "hard beats" used to indicate sections of the song. The "traditional method" consists of a pronounced strike by all singers every other beat. These may appear in the first or second line of a song, the end of a section, before the repetition of a song. A cluster of three hard beats (on consecutive beats) may be used at the end of a series of hard beats, while a few beats in the first line of a song indicate performer enthusiasm. In the "Hot Five" method five beats are used, with the first hard beat four beats before the second, after which the beats alternate.

Drum Etiquette

To understand drum protocol, a drum may be thought of as a person or being and is to be regarded and respected as such. Drum etiquette is highly important. There are regional variations. The drum is the central symbol of Oklahoma powwows and is located in the center of the dance floor and powwow (which are themselves shaped in concentric circles). Southern drums are suspended by four posts, one for each direction.

Northern drums are set up on the outside of the dance area, with the host drum in the best position. Musicians may not casually leave the drum, and it may never be left completely by itself till it is carried out at the end. People bring water to the drummers and generally assist the players as needed. The drum is offered gifts of tobacco during giveaways and musicians acknowledge this by standing.

Singing

While the drum is central to pow-wows, "the drum only helps them keep beat. Dancers key on the melody of the song. Rhythms, tones, pitch all help create their 'moves'." (p.85) Note that Bill Runs Above did not mention the lyrics of the songs, and while they are no doubt important, most lyrics of most songs employ vocables, syllable sounds such as "ya", "hey", and "loi". This is particularly evident in intertribal songs, such as the AIM Song, which cannot be biased towards a certain language.

The song structure consists of four pushups, singing the chorus and verse through four times. In each chorus the melody is introduced or led off by the lead singer whose is then seconded by another singer who begins to vary the melody before the end of the leader's first line. They are then joined by the entire chorus for the rest of the pushup. Three down strokes or hard beats mark the end of the chorus and beginning of the verse, and during these drummers while alter their dancing such as by hopping low like fancy dancers.

An increase in tempo and volume on the last five beats marks the end of the final verse. The dancing stops on the final beat and then a tail, or coda, finishes the song with a shortened chorus. Sometimes a drum group will sing the song more than four times, particularly when the song feels good and the singers cease the moment for an extra pushup or two (or more), or when a dancer blows a whistle or passes his staff or fan over the drum to signal that the song is to be continued four extra pushups while he prays.

Talented singers also sing off-the-beat, placing the words between the drum beats rather than on them, which "is probably the non-Indian's greatest obstacle in trying to learn Indian songs."

Genres and Change

In the 1970s drums had begun incorporating native words in addition to vocables. Groups such as the Black Lodge Singers have released songs with English words, such as on their children's albums. Given the inter-tribal style of pow wow music it may be viewed as less traditional or valuable though the music is also used to support tribal identity and display the value of a living culture.

Cakewalk

The Cakewalk dance was developed from a "Prize Walk" done in the days of slavery, generally at get-togethers on plantations in the Southern United States. Alternative names for the original form of the dance were "chalkline-walk", and the "walk-around". At the conclusion of a performance of the original form of the dance in an exhibit at the 1876 Centennial of the American Independence in Philadelphia, an enormous cake was awarded to the winning couple. Thereafter, it was performed in minstrel shows, exclusively by men until the 1890s. The inclusion of women in the cast "made possible all sorts of improvisations in the Walk, and the original was soon changed into a grotesque dance" which became very popular across the country.

AS A PLANTATION DANCE

The authors of "Jazz Dance: The Story of American Vernacular Dance" reported that an early 1950s experiment with African guests turned up "no worthy African counterpart" to the Cakewalk. While folklorist Harold Courlander reported that he had seen "certain passages" which were "virtually indistinguishable" from the Cakewalk in South Africa, Ghana and Nigeria, Brook Baldwin nevertheless wrote in 1981 that "Researchers have not yet pinpointed the origin of the cakewalk." One theory holds that the cakewalk originated as a parody of the formal ballroom dancing preferred of white slave owners, including satirical exaggerations of European dance moves.

First Person Accounts

In the 1981 article "The Cakewalk: A Study in Stereotype and Reality" Brooke Baldwin cites "an almost exhaustive compilation of those accounts which have been found so far". This compilation consists of eyewitness accounts by ex-slaves from Virginia and Georgia recorded by WPA researchers in the 1930s, along with second hand accounts from other sources. Baldwin notes that "when the researchers of the Federal Writer's Project of the WPA interviewed aged ex-slaves in the 1930s, there was no longer any need to suppress information about the happier moments of slave life."

Georgia Baker said that she sang a song when she was a child. "Walk light ladies, De cake's all dough" She laughed and added, "Us didn't know it when we was singin' dat tune to us chillun dat when us growed up us would be cakewalkin' to de same song".

Estella Jones: "Cakewalkin' was a lot of fun durin' slavery time. Dey swep yards real clearn and set benches for de party. Banjos wuz used for music makin'. De women's wor long, ruffled dresses wid hoops in 'em and de mens had on high hats, long split-tailed coasts, and some of em used walkin' sticks. De couple dat danced best got a prize. Sometimes de slave owners come to dese parties 'cause dey enjoyed watchin' de dance, and dey 'cided who danced de best. Most parties durin' slavery time, wuz give on Saturday night durin' work sessions, but durin' winter dey wuz give on most any night."

Second Hand, Oral Tradition Accounts

A South Carolinian told of Griffin, a fiddler who played for the dances of the whites as well as for the "annual cakewalks of his own people".

A story told to him by his childhood nanny in 1901 was repeated by 80 year old actor Leigh Whipple, "Us slave watched white folks' parties where the guests danced a minuet and then paraded in a grand march, with the ladies and gentlemen going different ways and then meeting again, arm in arm, and marching down the center together. Then we'd do it too, but we used to mock 'em every step. Sometimes the white folks noticed it, but they seemed to like it; I guess they thought we couldn't dance any better."

Ex-ragtime entertainer Shepard Edmonds told in 1950 of memories related to him by his parents from Tennessee; "...the cake walk was originally a plantation dance, just a happy movement they did to the banjo music because they couldn't stand still. It was generally on Sundays, when there was little work, that the slaves both young and old would dress up in hand-me-down finery to do a high-kicking, prancing walk-around. They did a take-off on the manners of the white folks in the "big house", but their masters, who gathered around to watch the fun, missed the point. It's supposed to be that the custom of a prize started with the master giving a cake to the couple that did the proudest movement."

Baldwin concludes that the Cakewalk was meant "to satirize the competing culture of supposedly 'superior' whites. Slaveholders were able to dismiss its threat in their own minds by considering it as a simple performance which existed for their own pleasure".

Written accounts by Tom Fletcher first published in 1954, were not addressed in the Baldwin article. Fletcher, who was born in 1873 and had a show business career beginning in 1888, wrote that when he was a child, his grandparents told him about the chalk-line walk/cakewalk, but they did not know when it started.

Fletcher's grandfather told him, "your grandmother and I, we won all the prizes and were taken from plantation to plantation. The dance became a great fad. It took skill and good nerves.The plantation is where shows like yours first started, son."

Fletcher adds that " The cake walk, in that section and at that time, was known as the chalk line walk. There was no prancing, just a straight walk on a path made by turns and so forth, along which the dancers made their way with a pail of water on their heads. The couple that was the most erect and spilled the least water or no water at all was the winner."

Fletcher also wrote, in another chapter of his book, that, "The old "chalk-line walk was revived with fancy steps by Charlie Johnson a clever eccentric dancer... The "chalk-line walk" then became known as the "Cake Walk."

"Cakewalk King" Charles E. Johnson related his grandmother's recollections of a dance-walk from "the old days". White folks from the big house carriaged down to watch their slaves couple off and do a dance-walk that was as elegant and poised as a Mozart minuet, but was flavored with an exaggerated grace that was sometimes comical. The cadenced walking and high stepping was usually supplied by a violin, a drum and a horn of some kind. A towering, extra sweet coconut cake was the prize for the winning couple. The cakewalk was still popular at the dances of ordinary folks after the Civil War.

ANOTHER THEORY

Ethel L. Urlin writing in the 1912 "Dancing, Ancient and Modern" stated that the cakewalk "originated in Florida, where it is said that the Negroes borrowed the idea of it from the war dances of the Seminole...The negroes were present as spectators at these dances, which consisted of wild and hilarious jumping and gyrating, alternating with slow processions in which the dancers walked solemnly in couples. The idea grew, and style in walking came to be practised among the negroes as an art."

The "Encyclopedia of Social Dance" echoed the Seminole Indian connection, stating that "Classes sprang up among the negroes for the teaching of the dance and the proper way to promenade" in the 1880s. As Florida developed into a winter resort, the dance became more performance oriented, and spread to Georgia, the Carolinas, Virginia, and finally New York.

CAKEWALK AS A POPULAR DANCE

An exhibit at the 1876 Philadelphia Centennial featured blacks singing folk songs and doing an old dance called the "chalk-line walk" in a plantation like setting. The dance was "done in the original fashion", as described by Fletcher. In 1877 performer-showmen Ernest Hogan and Edward Harrigan produced "Walking for Dat Cake, An Exquisite Picture of Negro Life and Customs" as a feature sketch at New York's Theater Comique on lower Broadway. Thereafter it was performed in minstrel shows, exlusively by men until the 1890s. In the 1893 production of "The Creole Show", which had opened in 1889, Dora Dean and her husband Charles E. Johnson made a hit dancing the cakewalk, their speciality, as partners.

During its run from 1889 through 1897, this show played to crowds in Boston and New York at the old Standard Theatre on Greeley Square, one of the first productions to discard blackface makeup. The production had a Negro cast with a chorus line of sixteen girls, and at a time when women on stage, and partner dancing on stage were something new. The inclusion of women in the cast "made possible all sorts of improvisations in the Walk, and the original was soon changed into a grotesque dance" which became very popular across the country.

A Grand Cakewalk was held in Madison Square Garden, the largest commercial venue in New York City, on February 17, 1892. The Illustrated London News carried a report of a barn dance in Ashtabula, Ohio in 1897 and written by an English woman traveller.

"The origin of that expression "taking the cake", had previously been an enigma to me, if I had ever thought about it before, but it was suddenly in an unexpected and most practical way (revealed to me)." Just before the ball was declared finished a long procession of couples was formed who walked in their very best manner around the room three times before the criticizing eyes of a dozen old people, who selected the best turned-out pair, and gravely presented them with a large plum cake.

In July 1898 the musical comedy "Clorindy The Origin of the Cakewalk" opened on Broadway in New York. Will Marion Cook wrote ragtime music for the show. Black dancers mingled with white cast members for the first instance of integration on stage in New York. Cook wrote, "My chorus sang like Russians, dancing meanwhile like Negroes, and cakewalking like angels, black angels! When the last note was sounded, the audience stood and cheered for at least ten minutes. This was the finale which Witmark had said no one would listen to. It was pandemonium... But did that audience take offense at my rags and lack of conducting polish? Not so you could notice it!"

"Dusky troopers march & cake walk" was written by Will Hardy and published in 1900. Sheet music covers for more cake walks can be viewed here.

Scott Joplin mentioned the cake walk in his folk ballet "The Ragtime Dance", published in 1902.

"Let me see you do the rag-time dance,

Turn left and do the cakewalk prance,

Turn the other way and do the slow drag -

Now take you lady to the World's Fair

And do the rag-time dance."

Performances of the "Cake Walk", including a "Comedy Cake Walk" were filmed by the American Motoscope & Biograph Co.in 1903. Prancing steps were the main steps shown in the "Cake Walk" segment, which featured two couples, and a solo dancer. All dancers were African American. 1903 was the same year that both the cakewalk and ragtime music arrived in Buenos Aires, Argentina. Leaning far forward or far backward is associated with defiance in Kongo. "We are palm trees, bent forward, bent back, but we never break." Another interpretations of these motions were "melting" to the beat, or protecting what is new (leaning forward) with the past (leaning back). The appearance of the cakewalk in Buenos Aires may have influenced influenced early styles of tango.

"Cakewalk King" Charles E. Johnson, who, with his wife Dora Jean, achieved fame cakewalking throughout the United States and Europe described his kind of dance as "simple, digified and well-dressed".

The Cake Walk was more fluid and imaginative than the established two-step, it was nevertheless a regularized form, more improvisational than its previous form, but highly formalized compared to later dances such as the Charleston, Black Bottom and Lindy Hop.

CAKEWALK AS A MUSICAL FORM

Most cakewalk music is notated in 2/4 time with two alternate heavy beats per bar, giving it an ooompah rhythm. The music was adopted into the works of various white composers, including Robert Russell Bennett, John Philip Sousa and Claude Debussy. Debussy wrote Golliwog's Cakewalk as the final movement of the Children's Corner suite (1908). The Cake Walk was an adapted and amended two-step, which had been spawned by the popularity of marches, most notably by John Philip Sousa.

Modern Times

The term "cakewalk" is often used to indicate something that is very easy or effortless. Though the dance itself could be physically demanding, it was generally considered a fun, recreational pastime. The phrase "takes the cake" also comes from this practice. Along the lines of this "easy or effortless" meaning, there is the modern Cakewalk (carnival game) which requires no dancing skill at all to win.

The term "cakewalk" has also been used to describe a game at a carnival or fair in which people walk around a numbered circle along to music. When the music is stopped, the caller draws a number from a jar and whoever is standing closest to that number wins a cake.

One version of the cakewalk is sometimes taught, performed included in competitions within the Highland Dance community, especially in the southern United States. In addition to the Highland Dance community, a version of the cakewalk seen in vintage film clips from the early 1900s is kept alive in the Lindy Hop community through performances by the Harlem Hot Shots and through cakewalk classes held in conjunction with Lindy Hop classes and workshops.

2 STRATEGY AND MANAGEMENT

Rural tourism related activities have been widely regarded as key-tools for rural development, especially in those countries where rural areas are in abundance as Romania and all East European countries where rural space and production is still a major part of whole economic structure, trying by this way to revitalize declining areas and ensure them possibilities of achieving a sustainable future.

At this purpose, rural tourism must be considered like a complex plurality of multi-faced activities, contributing both to growth of other activities in rural areas and to improvement of life quality for local inhabitants, all this as part of an effective rural development integrated system.

Due to necessary attraction of foreign currency in order to contribute in solving structural troubles of national economies in these countries, design of quite a lot of rural tourism activities on there has usually focused on international demand. However, and even when this could be perfectly right at a first stage, evidence for other countries shows that long-time maintenance of such activities requires of the existence of a basic infrastructure perhaps not so attractive, but indispensable internal market.

NEW ZEALAND TOURISM STRATEGY 2015

The New Zealand Tourism Strategy 2015 was launched by the Prime Minister, Rt Hon Helen Clark on 7 November 2007. The

Strategy updates the New Zealand Tourism Strategy 2010 that was launched in 2001.

The Tourism Strategy 2015 provides the vision, values and direction to lead the tourism sector into the future.

VALUES

Kaitiakitanga and Manaakitanga

The Strategy is underpinned by two key values, kaitiakitanga (guardianship) and manaakitanga (hospitality). These values provide the foundation for a sustainable approach to the development of our tourism industry. If we embrace these values, we will achieve our vision for 2015.

RESPONDING TO CHALLENGES

The Strategy responds to the significant changes that have occurred since 2001 in both the domestic and global environments in which tourism operates.

Changes at the global level include:

- growing concern about the impact of travel on climate change
- greater use of the internet and online bookings
- higher fuel prices.

At the domestic level, the industry faces challenges in:

- recruiting appropriately skilled staff
- becoming more environmentally sustainable
- the provision of appropriate, high quality infrastructure.

OUTCOMES

To guide the tourism industry towards its vision, the Strategy contains four outcomes:

1. NEW ZEALAND DELIVERS A WORLD-CLASS VISITOR EXPERIENCE

In a competitive international environment, it is vital that we capitalise fully on the many wonders New Zealand has to offer. We must deliver products that are high quality, authentic, unique and delivered with superb service.

2. NEW ZEALAND'S TOURISM SECTOR IS PROSPEROUS AND ATTRACTS ONGOING INVESTMENT

Our goals for the industry can only be realised if we can ensure continued profitability for those involved, and secure the investment required to continue upgrading our products.

3. THE TOURISM SECTOR TAKES A LEADING ROLE IN PROTECTING AND ENHANCING THE ENVIRONMENT

These actions are essential to protect tourism's greatest asset, and ensure the ongoing prosperity of our tourism industry.

4. THE TOURISM SECTOR AND COMMUNITIES WORK TOGETHER FOR MUTUAL BENEFIT

Tourism is a major economic contributor to many regions of the country. It is important that communities and operators build strong relationships and recognise each others' important contribution.

TARGETS

The Strategy sets out a number of ambitious targets. These focus on enhancing the value of tourism, and on quality tourism development.

ACTIONS AND PRIORITIES

A number of actions and priorities accompany each outcome. For these to be achieved, there will need to be cooperation between the private sector, central and local government, and other interest groups.

As with the 2010 Strategy, the development of New Zealand Tourism Strategy 2015 has been a combined effort between the private sector and government. It has been informed by extensive consultation with industry groups, local government, central government and interest groups. The next step is an implementation plan to be led by the Tourism Industry Association, Ministry of Tourism and Tourism New Zealand.

Tourism Strategy in Morocco

Tourism is the second largest foreign exchange earner in Morocco, after the phosphate industry.The Moroccan government is heavily investing in tourism development. A new tourism strategy called Vision 2010 was developed after the accession of King Mohammed VI in 1999. The government has targeted that Morocco will have 10 million visitors by 2010, with the hope that tourism will then have risen to 20% of GDP. A large government sponsored marketing campaigns to attract tourists advertised Morocco as a cheap and exotic, yet safe, place for European tourists.

Morocco's relatively high amount of tourists has been aided by its location, tourist attractions, and relatively low price. Cruise ships visit the ports of Casablanca and Tangier. Morocco is close to Europe and attracts visitors to its beaches. Because of its proximity to Spain, tourists in southern Spain's coastal areas take one- to three-day trips to Morocco. Air services between Morocco and Algeria have been established, many Algerians have gone to Morocco to shop and visit family and friends.

Morocco is relatively inexpensive because of the devaluation of the dirham and the increase of hotel prices in Spain. Morocco has an excellent road and rail infrastructure that links the major cities and tourist destinations with ports and cities with international airports. Low-cost airlines offer cheap flights to the country.

Tourism in Morocco is well developed, with a strong tourist industry focused on the country's coast, culture, and history.

Morocco has been one of the most politically stable countries in North Africa, which has allowed tourism to develop. The Moroccan government created a Ministry of Tourism in 1985.

In the second half of the 1980s and the early 1990s, between 1 and 1.5 million Europeans visited Morocco. Most of these visitors were French or Spanish, with about 100,000 each from Britain, Germany, and the Netherlands. Tourists mostly visited large beach resorts along the Atlantic coast, particularly Agadir. About 20,000 people from Saudi Arabia visited, some of who bought holiday homes.

Receipts from tourism fell by 16.5% in 1990, the year the Gulf War began. In 1994, Algeria closed its border with Morocco after being falsely accused of the Marrakech attack, this caused the number of Algerian visitors to fall considerably; there were 70,000 visitors in 1994 and 13,000 in 1995, compared to 1.66 million in 1992 and 1.28 million in 1993.

In 2008 there were 8 million tourist arrivals, compared with about 7.4 million in 2007 i.e. a 7% growth compared to 2007 30% of the tourists in 2008 were one of the 3:8 million Moroccans living abroad. Most of the visitors to Morocco continue to be European, with French people making up almost 20% of its all visitors. Most Europeans visit in April and the autumn, apart from the Spanish, who mostly visit in June and August.

PLAN AZUR

The "Plan Azur", is a large scale project initiated by king Mohammed VI, is meant to internationalise Morocco. The plan provides for creating six coastal resorts for holiday-home owners and tourists (five on the Atlantic coast and one on the Mediterranean), the daily telegraph noted. The plan also includes other large-scale development projects such as upgrading regional airports to attract budget airlines, and building new train and road links.

Thus, the country achieved an 11% cent rise in tourism in the first five months of 2008 compared with the same period last year, it said, adding that French visitors topped the list with 927,000 followed by Spaniards (587,000) and Britons (141,000). Morocco, which is close to Europe, has a mix of culture and the exotic that makes it popular with Europeans buying holiday homes.

While Morocco was a French Protectorate (from 1912 to 1956) tourism was focused on urban areas such as the Mediterranean cities of Tangier and Casablanca. Tangier attracted many writers, such as Jack Kerouac and William S. Burroughs. There was a period of beach resort development at places such as Agadir on the Atlantic coast in the 1970s and 1980s.

Tourism is increasingly focused on Morocco's culture, such as its ancient cities. The modern tourist industry capitalizes on Morocco's ancient Roman and Islamic sites, and on its landscape and cultural history. 60% of Morocco's tourists visit for its culture and heritage. The country's attractions can be divided into seven regions: Tangier and the surrounding area; Agadir and its beach resorts; Marrakech; Casablanca; the Imperial cities; Ouarzazate; and Tarfaya and its beach resorts.

Agadir is a major coastal resort and has a third of all Moroccan bed nights. It is a base for tours to the Atlas Mountains. Other resorts in north Morocco are also very popular. Casablanca is the major cruise port in Morocco, and has the best developed market for tourists in Morocco. Marrakech in central Morocco is a popular tourist destination, but is more popular among tourists for one- and two-day excursions that provide a taste of Morocco's history and culture. The Majorelle botanical garden in Marrakech is a popular tourist attraction. It was bought by the fashion designer Yves Saint-Laurent and Pierre Bergé in 1980. Their presence in the city helped to boost the city's profile as a tourist destination.

Follow in the footsteps of Lawrence of Arabia and hike the majestic mountains of Wadi Rum, or see an Arcadian landscape of rural communities farming the same land that their families have for centuries by wandering the Al Ayoun Trail. Walking can take you closer to this beautiful land and people.

Walking trails in Jordan include Al Ayoun Trail, Dana Village Trail, Jabal Amman to Jabal Luweibdeh, and the Soap Maker's Trail, all of which are detailed below

Al Ayoun Trail

Where?

The Al Ayoun Trail meanders through the mountainous and verdant agricultural communities of Rasun, Orjan and Baoun in northern Jordan. It is a twelve kilometre walk that takes you through villages that have held communities for countless generations, and past fields tilled since biblical and Bronze Age times.

Timeless

Carefully cultivated for all those years, the whole area is painted with the rich green foliage of family-owned olive groves and well-tended orchards of apricot, cherry, pomegranate, fig and almond trees. Some of the olive trees have served the families here for so long that they are as gnarled and stout as ancient European oaks.

Water

Water is a scarce and precious resource in Jordan, but this area is blessed with a number of springs that gush from the rocks at the base of the steep wadi cliffs.

The water is carefully carried away in narrow, babbling irrigation canals to feed the thirsty market gardens and orchards. In the past, the water was also used for power, running seven mills; the ruins of some can still be seen.

"There are more than thirteen natural springs in the area. Because of the water, here it is always green"

Mahmoud Hawawreh

Culture

Each of the three villages en route has its own story; Baoun was the birthplace of Aisha al Baouniya, a pre-eminent female Islamic scholar of the 15th century. The forests around Rasun are dotted with dolmens, mysterious Bronze Age burial chambers. Orjan has a Christian tradition dating back to the birth of the religion and still has a Christian community today.

Abraham Trail

The Al Ayoun Trail is one section of an international walking route that attempts to recreate the trek undertaken by Prophet Abraham, a key figure in Muslim, Christian and Jewish faiths.

Dana Village Trail

Ecology

Of all the nature reserves in Jordan, Dana is special. Not only is it the country's largest, it also has an incredibly diverse biosphere. From the lofty, rugged cliff tops of the Great Rift Valley, down 1700 meters to the desert of Wadi Arabia, Dana's territory passes through four distinct eco-zones giving it a wealth of diverse plant, animal and birdlife.

Scenery

It is saturated with stunning views. Stood at the very lip of the Great Rift Valley you can look down through the snaking near-vertical wadis towards the desert far below. At sunset it seems as though you are stood at the edge of the world.

"Dana is a treasure. I love it. I was born and grew up here but every day and every moment you feel it is different. I watch the sunset and sunrise. I feel like a person who has come here for the first time"

Abdullah Hwaldeh, Dana Guest House Duty Manager

History

Dana village perches like an eagle's nest at the brink of the precipicc. Its natural defences, fertile soil and springs have made it an ideal home for human communities for over 4000 years. In recent years the picturesque, honey-coloured, rock-built houses of Dana village have been slowly abandoned as families left in search of jobs elsewhere.

New Life

An innovative project by a group called Friends of Dana and the work of the Royal Society for the Conservation of Nature has breathed new life into this community. Tourism has brought jobs and local people are returning to make Dana their home once more.

Tour

The Village Trail explores the narrow alleyways of Dana with glimpses through door-less entrances into abandoned houses, past local people sitting on their doorsteps and out into the terraced fields where olive trees, herbs and crops are still grown.

This is just one of several walks that start from three accommodation sites in Dana Reserve.

Jabal Amman to Jabal Luweibdeh

Amman is a city on hills, originally seven, now around twenty. The areas of the city take their names from the hills they are built on. Although Amman is a large, modern, busy capital, it is possible to find quiet backstreets to wander through on foot.

The Two Hills

Two areas of Amman that lend themselves well to walking and exploring are Jabel Amman and Jabal Luweibdeh - 'jabal' is hill in Arabic. Both have narrow streets that snake around the hills following their contours, interconnected with steps and quiet alleys descending straight down the fall line. Both have strong cultural and artistic quarters with galleries, coffee shops, craft shops and historical buildings.

"There are a couple of neighbourhoods, Jabal Amman, Jabal Luweibdeh... that are gaining momentum as cultural hotspots"

Safa Hijazeen

Jabal Amman

On Jabal Amman the focal point is Wild Jordan. This is the superbly designed headquarters of the Royal Society for the Conservation of Nature, RSCN, a real architectural gem with a restaurant offering delicious views and innovative menus plus a gift shop that sells high quality crafts from all of the small scale artisan projects the society supports.

Jabal Luweibdeh

The epicentre of Jabal Luweibdeh is Darat al Funun, an art centre of international reputation housed in atmospheric and elegant 1920's buildings, with a cafe, gallery space, gardens and an outdoor sculpture studio.

Guides

There is a guidebook with a map of Jabal Luweibdeh called "My Neighbourhood" by Saleem Ayoub Quna and the RSCN has a pamphlet with route for a suggested walk around Jabal Amman

Walking and Trekking

As of 2006, activity and adventure tourism in the Atlas and Rif Mountains are the fastest growth area in Moroccan tourism. These locations have excellent walking and trekking opportunities from late March to mid-November. The government is investing in trekking circuits. They are also developing desert tourism in competition with Tunisia.

For small rural communities, business attraction is what is going to save us. Our once charming, bustling downtowns are lined with vacant storefronts, and in too many towns our young people are heading to the big city.

We still have our compelling small town atmosphere, our authentic experiences and outdoor recreation that brings people to many of our towns on the weekends.

Hiking vs. Trekking

	Hiking	Trekking
Equipment:	Depends on the weather, day or over-night hiking. Shoes applicable to the hiking terrain, water, compass, sometimes a hiking pole. Backpack with survival kit, food and medicine for overnight hiking.	Survival kit, camping gear, boots, compass, clothing applicable to changes in temperature especially if in mountainous areas.
Overview:	An outdoor activity of walking in natural environments often on pre charted paths called hiking trails.	A long journey on non-designated paths which could last several days and could be challenging. It is more intense and energetic than hiking.
Worldwide differences:	Hiking is called by different names around the world: tramping in New Zealand, bush-walking in Australia, trekking in Nepal.	Trekking is also known as backpacking but should not be confused with mountaineering
Holidays:	Day hiking or walking holidays are popular in Europe, New Zealand, Chile, Costa Rica, Hawaii and North America.	Trekking is popular in the Himalayan foothills in Nepal, India and Bhutan. The Andes in South America is also popular trekking Mecca.

Contd....

Environmental impact:	Hikers over many years in an area can destroy the natural environment they walk in through wood gathering, fires, fecal matter, leaving non-biodegradable matter.	As treks take longer than hikes, the environmental impact can be greater.
Locations:	Usually in beautiful natural environments, nature trails, hills.	In areas where there is no means of transport and areas of great natural beauty. Usually

3 Rural Tourism Policy

Tourism in rural areas is governed by a range of policies from a number of organizations. Due to the unique nature of the rural tourism product these policies must cover issues as far reaching as farming, agriculture and health.

The development of rural tourism in the last two decades and the experience that Romania has achieved in this area have drawn the attention of researchers and academics from the country and from abroad and together with the managers of tourist and agritourist guesthouses they attempt to provide solutions to the problems, numerous and difficult, facing tourism.

Tourism is becoming increasingly important to the U.S. economy. A conservative estimate from the Federal Reserve Board in Kansas, based on 2000 data, shows that basic travel and tourism industries accounted for 3.6 percent of all U.S. employment. Even more telling, data from the Travel Industry Association of America indicate that one out of every 18 people in the U.S. has a job directly resulting from travel expenditures.

The importance of tourism to local economies varies across the U.S. Some places have an enormous investment in the tourist industry, while others lag far behind. In Nevada, for example, nearly 28 percent of jobs are related to this industry, but in Alabama travel and tourist employment is less than 2 percent.

Recently, tourism has emerged as a major economic activity that is employment oriented and earns foreign exchange. Its share in the worlds GDP in 1994-95 was 10% which is more than the world military budgets put together. In global terms, the investment in tourism industry and travel trade accounts for 7% of the total capital investment.

Nowadays, 21.2 crore people around the globe are employed in travel trade and tourism. In future, this industry is likely to see unprecedented growth. According to the World Tourism Council at Bruseels, the revenues from travel and tourism in Asia Pacific region will grow at the rate of 7.8% annually over the next decade.

Nevertheless, the future of tourism is full of potential for small business owners. With the increases in security concerns for international travel and travel to large metro areas, many rural tourist companies are moving in with their own offerings. Many of these low-risk rural areas may be able to rely on tourism as an important part of their economy. Maine—where more than 40 percent of small and home-based businesses are involved in some kind of tourist enterprise—is a good example of this.

A wide variety of tourist opportunities exist throughout rural America and continue to grow as increasing numbers of local entrepreneurs identify new ways to market previously untapped local resources and attractions, and bring tourists into their area.

Moreover, the nature of tourism is especially well-suited to small-scale rural enterprises. Many remote areas are ideal locations for nature-based activities like hunting and fishing, or ecotourism activities such as hiking and rafting.

Travellers interested in local cultures and the heritage of places they visit find an added benefit in having the town's local history buff lead a tour through the battlefield, or in the personal touches of a small bed and breakfast. Agri-tourism (farm-based tourism) invites tourists to experience working ranches, hay rides, corn mazes, pumpkin patches, and much more.

Through land-grant universities and other partners, NIFA promotes research, education, and outreach activities that expand opportunities for rural tourism. Since 1998, NIFA competitive and formula grants have supported 65 research projects, including studies on the importance of local infrastructure in developing a tourist industry, attitudes towards tourism among local populations, and how best to promote local amenities without over-exploitation.

Since 1994, the National Extension Tourism Design Team has identified and promoted extension tourism programs across the U.S. This team's responsibilities and achievements include a list of Extension Tourism Faculty by state and expertise, as well as the annual National Extension Tourism Conference. The Design Team also maintains a National Tourism Publication database published through Michigan State University Extension.

Funded by a grant from NIFA, a major outreach project called "Adding Value to Agriculture: A Collaborative Approach Based on Agricultural Tourism" is promoting partnerships among growers, marketers, and community representatives to explore and develop new agritourism markets.

A productive partnership between state specialists, local extension staff and resource conservation and development officials has allowed Elliott County, KY, once one of the poorest areas in the nation, to become a thriving center for eco-heritage tourism. Gwenda Adkins, local county extension agent, notes that "the knowledge and skills that helped Elliott County came through tourism internship programs and continued support from specialists at the University of Kentucky."

Through Sea Grant, a partnership between the nation's universities and the National Oceanic and Atmospheric Administration, recreation and tourism extension specialists across the U.S. educate coastal residents, business owners, and community leaders about coastal recreation and tourism and work with coastal communities to expand tourism opportunities.

Information and expertise on marine recreation and related subjects can be found on the Oregon State Web site. In addition, the National Sea Grant Library at the University of Rhode Island offers a searchable database of ocean and coastal research and outreach publications from all over the U.S., many of them available online.

Below is an overview of those documents which have an impact on the South East's rural tourism sector, these include documents written on both a national and regional basis. South East England Development Agency (SEEDA) devotes a chapter to building a "World Class Rural Economy". This involves resolving the tension between conservation and economic growth, stating that this must be a priority.

Economic development must be seen as a means of maintaining and enhancing the region's natural assets. This will only be achieved if measures to tackle economic, social and environmental issues are integrated, both in design and delivery.

The OECD Development Centre occupies a unique place within the OECD and in the international community. It is the place that brings the Organization for Economic Co-operation and Development (OECD) and the developing world together.

The Centre is a forum where countries come to share their mutual experience of economic and social development policies. The Centre contributes expert analysis and studies to the development policy deliberations and debates. The objective is to help decision makers find policy solutions to stimulate growth and improve living conditions in developing and emerging countries.

The Centre's homepage defines the Centre's mission in the following one sentence: "The OECD Development Centre helps policy makers in OECD and developing countries find innovative solutions to the global challenges of development, poverty alleviation and the curbing of inequality."

We measures the impact of changing economic conditions in OECD countries on tourist arrivals to countries/destinations in Latin America and the Caribbean. A model of utility maximization across labor, consumption of goods and services at home, and consumption of tourism services across monopolistically competitive destinations abroad is presented.

The model yields estimable equations arrivals as a function of OECD economic conditions and the elasticity of substitution across tourist destinations. Estimates suggest median tourism arrivals decline by at least three to five percent in response to a one percent increase in OECD unemployment, even after controlling for declines in OECD consumption and output gaps.

Arrivals to individual destination are driven by differing exposure to OECD country groups sharing similar business cycle characteristics. Estimates of the elasticity of substitution suggest that tourism demand is highly price sensitive, and that a variety of costs to delivering tourism services drive market share losses in uncompetitive destinations.

One recent cost change, the 2009 easing of restrictions on U.S. travel to Cuba, supported a small (countercyclical) boost to Cuba's arrivals of U.S. non-family travel, as well as a pre-existing surge in family travel (of Cuban origin). Despite the US becoming Cuba's second highest arrival source, Cuban policymakers have significant scope for lowering the relatively high costs of family travel from the United States.

WORLD TRAVEL AND TOURISM COUNCIL

The World Travel & Tourism Council (WTTC) was conceptualized in the early 1980s when a group of CEOs came to the realization that although Travel & Tourism was the largest service industry in the world and the biggest provider of jobs, nobody knew it. There was no consolidated data or voice for the industry to give the message to elected official and policy makers.

WTTC was established in 1990 and today the Council is positioned as the global business leaders' forum for Travel & Tourism, comprising the Chairmen and Chief Executives of 100 of the world's foremost organizations, representing all regions and sectors of the industry; a membership list is attached.

Awareness

WTTC works to raise awareness of Travel & Tourism as one of the world's largest industries, employing approximately 235 million people and generating 9.3 per cent of world GDP, WTTC works together with governments to raise awareness of the economic and social importance of the industry across the world.

WTTC's mission focuses on three main areas:

Driving the Agenda: Raising awareness of the impact of Travel & Tourism and working with governments to make the industry an economic and job-creating priority

The Facilitator: Helping industry participants to understand, anticipate, interpret and act on global key regional development

The Networking Forum: WTTC is the business leaders' forum to which Travel & Tourism players aspire

Blueprint for New Tourism

By 2003, events around the world such as the September 11th attacks, war in Iraq, the SARS crisis and increased terrorism meant that WTTC had to work to rebuild confidence among travellers. The Global Travel & Tourism Summit in 2003 was opened up to global press and media for the first time and the theme – Building New Tourism – came out of the atmosphere at the time. The outcome of the Summit shaped the Council's future vision and led to the launch of the Blueprint for New Tourism.

The Blueprint for New Tourism provides a new strategic framework to ensure that Travel & Tourism works for everyone in the future. It promotes Travel & Tourism as a partnership between the private and public sectors, matching the needs of economies, local and regional authorities and local communities with those of business.

The three main messages that form the framework for the Blueprint for New Tourism are: (a) Governments recognizing Travel & Tourism as a top priority. (b) Business balancing economics with people, culture and environment. (c) A shared pursuit of long-term growth and prosperity.

WTTC Research

When the World Travel & Tourism Council (WTTC) was established in 1990, the founding Members decided that the quantification of Travel & Tourism's impact on world and national economies would be the most important contribution they could make to achieve their goal of raising awareness among policy leaders and decision-makers of Travel & Tourism's economic contribution and its potential for creating wealth and employment around the world.

The subsequent 19 years of investment in research made a significant contribution to the development of the new international standard for Tourism Satellite Accounting (TSA) research, adopted in 2001 by the United Nations Statistical Commission. WTTC has also developed a Crisis Impact Forecasting Model to assess the potential impact of a crisis on the industry within 48 hours. It was put into place following the crises of the London and Egypt bombings in 2005.

TSA Commissioned Reports

Over the years, WTTC and its research partner, UK-based Oxford Economics (OE), have endeavoured to create a system of Tourism Satellite Accounting research, which now covers 181 economies around the world. Using a combination of macro-economic research and forecasts, national accounting data/ information, Travel & Tourism variables and econometric modelling, WTTC/OE have produced a system of research covering many concepts of Travel & Tourism 'Demand', from personal consumption to business purchases, capital investment, government spending and exports.

This information is then translated into economic concepts of production, such as gross domestic product (GDP) and employment, which can be compared with other industries and the economy as a whole to provide statistical information that can assist in policy- and business decision-making. Today, WTTC produces annual TSA forecasts for 181 countries and thirteen regions and carries out commissioned TSA reports for a growing number of countries, regions, and cities each year..

Regional Initiatives

WTTC has established two Regional Initiatives in India and China and is now working more extensively in China. Due to a consensus from Members of the Council, a Middle East Chapter has been founded to work together on region-specific issues, and similarly in Europe, an EU Steering Committee has been meeting regularly to drive WTTC's lobbying in Brussels. The purpose of these initiatives is to bring together key players from across the region to work together to accelerate industry growth.

Policy Reports and Initiatives

The Council works with and consults with its Members to produce policy papers covering a wide variety of topical issues facing the industry. These papers are produced with the aim of presenting the Council's collective stance and putting forward guidelines on how to best meet challenges or optimize opportunities.

WTTC's Policy statements can be region-specific or globally applicable, setting out strategies for areas of business ranging from corporate social responsibility to tackling infrastructure, human resources, and climate change. WTTC also launched the Green Globe environmental awareness programme which became an autonomous organization in 1998.

Global Travel & Tourism Summit

The Global Travel & Tourism Summit is an annual WTTC gathering for both public and private sector leaders of travel and tourism. The Summit aims to facilitate meaningful dialogue among the world's Travel & Tourism industry and government leaders. Past locations of the Summit include Vilamoura, Doha, New Delhi, Washington D.C., Lisbon, and Dubai. The 9th Global Travel & Tourism Summit took place from 14-16 May 2009 in Florianópolis, Brazil.

Tourism for Tomorrow Awards

The Tourism for Tomorrow Awards were set up in 1989 by the Federation of Tour Operators to encourage action from all sectors of the industry to protect the environment. WTTC took over the Awards in 2004. Awarded annually, they recognise and promote the world's leading examples of best practice in responsible tourism development across four categories:

Destination Stewardship Award, Conservation Award, Community Benefit Award, Global Tourism Business Award. Winners and finalists are taking the stage in a Awards special session during WTTC's Global Travel & Tourism Summit.

TRAVEL FACTS AND STATISTICS

Additional information regarding U.S. Travel studies, travel trends and more can be found in Research. Looking for data on the economic impact of travel in the U.S.? Be sure to visit PowerofTravel.org, an information-rich online hub containing economic travel data and information on travel's significant impact on the U.S. workforce and economy.

NEW! The new **U.S. Travel Answer Sheet** is filled with facts and statistics about the travel industry and its impact on the U.S. economy. Download this one-page fact sheet about a leading American industry that's more than just fun.

Activities with the greatest level of interest among U.S. adults are, in order, visiting friends and relatives, sightseeing, beaches/ waterfronts, visiting zoos/aquariums/science museums, national parks, visiting a state park, going on a cruise, theme parks, visiting a city and visiting a mountain area. Interest in the engaging in the activities varies by generation, household income, gender and most other demographic characteristics of leisure travelers. (Source: travelhorizons™, July 2009)

Air is the secondary means of transportation used by leisure visitors who traveled for leisure purposes between August 2008 and July 2009. (Source: travelhorizons™, July 2009)

Air travel: About 42 percent of U.S. adults reported traveling by air for leisure trips taken between August 2008 and July 2009. The percentage of air travelers increases to 48 percent among U.S. adults who traveled for business purposes in the past year. (Source: travelhorizons™, July 2009)

Air travel hassles: A June 2008 study by the U.S. Travel Association revealed a deep frustration among air travelers that caused them to avoid an estimated 41 million trips over the past 12 months at a cost of more than $26 billion to the U.S. economy. Air travelers expressed little optimism for positive change, with nearly 50 percent saying that the air travel system is not likely to improve in the near future. The effect of avoided trips cost airlines more than $9 billion in revenue; hotels nearly $6 billion and restaurants more than $3 billion. Federal, state and local governments lost more than $4 billion in tax revenue because of reduced spending by travelers. (Source: Air Travel Survey, 2008)

Auto is the primary means of transportation used by leisure visitors (76%) who traveled for leisure purposes between August 2008 and July 2009. The percentage of leisure visitors traveling by auto varies by income, generation and other demographic characteristics. (Source: travelhorizons™, July 2009)

Business travel in the U.S. is responsible for $246 billion in spending and 2.3 million American jobs; $100 billion of this spending and 1 million American jobs are linked directly to meetings and events. For every dollar invested in business travel, businesses experience an average $12.50 in increased revenue and $3.80 in new profits. A 10 percent increase in business travel spending would increase multi-factor productivity, leading to a U.S. GDP increase between 1.5 percent and 2.8 percent. (Source: The Return on Investment of U.S. Business Travel)

Business travel in the U.S. remains flat compared to the same period last year with only one-in-five U.S. adults still expecting to take business trips in the next six months. However, the number of business trips expected to be taken in the next 6 months has increased slightly to 3.9. (Source: travelhorizons™, July 2009)

Canada and Mexico travelers represented over 56% of all international visitors to the U.S. in 2008. In 2008, 18.9 million Canadians and 13.7 million Mexicans visited the U.S., and combined they spent more than $22 billion on travel in the U.S. (Source: IVIS)

China has been a fast-growing market of international travelers to the U.S. since the United States and China signed a Memorandum of Understanding in 2007 that opened the doors for promotion of travel to the entire U.S. In 2008, almost 500,000 thousand Chinese traveled to the U.S., staying on average 23 nights and spending $7,200 per visit.Total spending by Chinese travelers in the U.S. was $3.5 billion in 2008. By 2013, visitation from China to the U.S. is expected to grow 61% over 2008 arrivals — rising from 493,000 in 2008 to a forecasted 795,000 in 2013. (Source: IVIS China Summary, Office of Travel and Tourism Industries)

Environmental issues impact travel decisions. With over 79% of U.S. adults considering themselves environmentally-conscious and increasingly aware of terms such as carbon footprint and global warming, travelers are beginning to make decisions based on sustainability criteria. However, while environmental responsibility is one of the prime factors influencing the selection of travel companies, American travelers continue to lack the willingness to pay extra to support environmentally-friendly travel providers. (Source: travelhorizonsTM, July 2009)

Family travelers, those traveling with either children or grandchildren, make up 30% of U.S. adult leisure travelers. Grandparents traveling with grandchildren represent 7% of U.S. adult leisure travelers. Family travelers take an average of 4.5 trips each year. (Source: travelhorizonsTM, July 2009)

Gen X (those born from 1965 through 1980) makes up 31 percent of all leisure travelers and 36 percent of all business travelers. Gen Xers take an average of 3.5 leisure trips and 6.9 business trips per year.

Gen Y (those born after 1980) makes up 12 percent of all U.S. leisure travelers and those traveling in this group take and average of 3.9 leisure trips per year. Gen Yers also represent 13 percent of all business travelers and take an average of 4.2 business trips per year.

The Hispanic/Latino population in the U.S. is expected to reach 47.8 million by 2010 or 16 percent of the total population. By 2050, the Hispanic/Latino population is projected to total 102.6 million, comprising 24 percent of the U.S. population. In 2007, there were an estimated 16.2 million Hispanic adult leisure travelers who took a combined 50.4 million domestic and outbound trips and spent $58.7 billion on their travels. (Source: Profile of Hispanic/Latino Leisure Travelers, 2008 Edition)

International travel to the United States is one of the nation's leading exports. In 2008, 58 million international travelers visited the U.S., up 4% from 2007. Total spending (excluding passenger fares) from all international visitors in the U.S. was $110.4 billion in 2008, an increase of 14% over 2007. In 2008, the top five overseas markets for travelers to the U.S. were the U.K. with 4.5 million arrivals, Japan with 3.2 million arrivals and Germany with 1.8 million arrivals, France with 1.2 million arrivals, and Italy with 780 thousand arrivals. Unfortunately, although international travel has boomed over the past several years, with 48 million more overseas trips taken in 2008 than in 2000, America actually lost visitors, welcoming 633,000 fewer overseas travelers in 2008. If the United States had simply kept pace with global travel trends, 58 million more overseas travelers would have visited the United States between 2000 and 2008 – and would have generated an estimated 245,000 new U.S. jobs in 2008 alone. (Source: IVIS, www.poweroftravel.org)

The Internet was used by approximately 90 million American adults to plan travel during the past year with 76 percent of online travelers planning leisure trips online. Most online travel planners are somewhat or extremely satisfied with their experiences in using the Internet to plan their trips. Importantly, most see the Internet as a very useful or essential tool for planning many/most aspects of a trip including where to stay overnight, planning travel routes, potential places to visit, attractions to visit, as well as learning about what to do. The primary tools for travel planning are online travel agency websites, search engines, company websites and destination websites. Airline tickets, overnight lodging accommodations and car rentals are the dominant travel products and services purchased online by travel planners. (Source: Travelers' Use of the Internet, 2009)

Mature travelers (those born before1946) represent 21 percent of all leisure travelers and those who travel in this group take an average of 4.1 leisure trips each year. The Mature Group also comprises 14 percent of business travelers. Mature business travelers take an average of 6.7 business trips each year.

Older boomers (those born from 1946 through 1954) make up 15 percent of leisure travelers and take an average of 4.4 leisure trips each year. Older Boomers also represent 16 percent of all business travelers and these travelers take an average of 10.1 business trips each year.

Online travel planners have increased many facets of trip planning including the number of information sources used for planning, the number of places considered during the planning process and the number of places actually visited. The Internet has also led to decreases in the extent to which travelers make calls, especially to a travel agency or airline, state and local tourism office, car rental agency, or hotel. (Source: Travelers' Use of the Internet, 2009)

Pets make great travel companions. Over 49 percent of U.S. adult leisure travelers consider their pet to be part of the family and 18 percent of U.S. adult leisure travelers usually take their pets with them when they travel. (Source: travelhorizons™, July 2009)

Solo travelers, those who travel alone with no companions, comprise 11% of all U.S. adult leisure travelers. Solo travelers take slightly fewer trips per year (4.3) than those who travel with other adults (4.8). (Source: travelhorizons™, July 2009)

Travel planning sources: The most widely-used information source to plan leisure trips is the Internet followed by online travel agencies, branded suppliers, and other websites. One-in four of adult leisure travelers also obtain information from friends, relatives, neighbors, and/or co-workers. Guide books were the fifth most popular source, being used by 15 percent of all leisure travelers. (Source: travelhorizons™, July 2009)

Young boomers (those born from 1955 through 1964) represent 21 percent of all U.S. leisure travelers and 22 percent of business travelers. Young Boomers also take an average of 4.1 leisure trips and 5.6 business trips per year.

TOURISM POLICY OF THE SWISS CONFEDERATION

- Compilation of the report of the Federal Council of 26.05.1996 on the gouvernment's tourismus policy, concentrating in particular on the creation of optimum framework conditions for Swiss tourism (e.g. the granting of a special value added tax rate for the hotel trade and other tourism-related accommodation)
- Implementation of the Swiss tourism concept of 21.03.1981 for an environment-friendly regional planning in the context of tourism.

TOURISM PROMOTION AND THE PROGRAMME OF THE SWISS CONFEDERATION

Swiss Hotel Loan Company

The Swiss Hotel Loan Company is a federal government public-sector co-operative with its head office in Zürich. It is subject to supervision by the Federal Department of the Economic Affairs and the State Secretariat for Economic Affairs (SECO).

The SGH grants subordinated loans to accommodation businesses in tourist areas on advantageous terms. In addition, the company operates a consultancy department, offering fee-paid consultancy services to the accommodation industry.

ST Tourism Switzerland

Tourism Switzerland is a public-sector body with its head office in Zürich. The organisation is subject to supervision by the Federal Department of Economic Affairs and the State Secretariat for Economic Affairs (SECO).

The principal task of Tourism Switzerland is to promote Switzerland as a destination country for travel and tourism.

Tourism Switzerland has established itself as a national marketing and sales organisation for Switzerland as a travel destination and a location for holidays and conferences. In maintains branch offices in the most important countries from which tourists originate, in order to provide in-the-spot marketing for Switzerland as a tourist destination.

Helping Rural Tourism

Over the past 4 years we have undertaken a series of projects for the South East Regional Tourist Board, Tourism South East.

Rural tourism projects include:

- A B&B sector study, identifying issues and opportunities for the B&Bs, together with a toolkit to help local authorities support B&Bs in their areas
- New product development of 'health and well-being' rural visitor experiences, together with business guidance materials
- Delivering seminars to rural pubs and B&Bs on business development
- Preparing business guidance materials for those looking to establish a B&B or self-catering business
- Preparing data and intelligence to feed into local authority Local Development Framework policy drafting

- Researching the farm-based B&B sector

We have also worked with a number of county and local authorities to improve the networking, communication, knowledge and skills in the B&B and self-catering sectors.

Our services to rural tourism include:

- Market research and intelligence
- Competitor analysis
- New product development
- Feasibility studies
- Investment appraisal
- Problem solving
- Compiling evidence and argument to support planning applications
- Preparing business plans
- Marketing and promotion strategy, and directing businesses towards effective promotion solutions
- Quality assurance schemes
- Raising finance including grant aid
- Legal and regulatory advice
- Networking businesses into the local tourism support networks
- Performance improvement
- Budgeting and performance monitoring
- Audits of supply
- Development of data and intelligence to support local, regional and national tourism policy formulation
- Training and continuous professional development workshops and seminars for rural accommodation providers

Rural Tourism Occupancies Falling Fast Across Scotland

TOURISM operators in rural Scotland have seized on new data showing a marked fall in guest-house bed occupancy in most of the country as evidence that VisitScotland is "failing the rural economy".

Alan Keith, who leads the Association of Dumfries and Galloway Accommodation Providers, and is an established critic of the tourism agency, cited a survey carried out by TNS for VisitScotland, for the first six months of 2006 that showed bed occupancy rates in the grass roots B&B and guest-house sector have dropped across some of Scotland's most popular areas, including Ayrshire and Arran, Argyll and Perthshire.

This was despite occupancy figures for Edinburgh rising by 4 per cent in the same period. The rural figures had previously risen each year since 2002.

Citing the fact that all areas of rural Scotland, excepting Fife, the Borders, the Western Isles and Orkney, saw occupancy decreases, Keith said: "These results support our contention that VisitScotland's policy is harming rural areas more than urban regions, and casts doubt on their ambitious target of a 50 per cent increase in tourism by 2001 which look unlikely to be achieved. If their policy is to increase city tourism irrespective of how much it damages rural areas, then that cannot be supported."

Keith said that he had been bombarded with messages of support from others across Scotland.

The TNS January-June 2006 figures come hot on the hells of a major change in the statistical measurement of Scottish and UK tourism growth since 2004.

Statistics of visitors to Scotland from elsewhere in Britain (known as "domestic visitors"), who account for around 86 per cent of the entire Scottish tourism market, were drastically downgraded earlier this year, after the UK Tourism Survey changed its methodology to give "a more accurate picture".

While the changes in the way the survey is conducted makes direct comparison between visitors figures before and after 2005 impossible, they nevertheless reveal that domestic visitors were actually contributing £700 million less to the Scottish economy in 2005, than previously believed (£3 billion rather than £3.7bn).

The overall tourism spend for all tourists in 2005 was £4.2bn, or £500m less than the discredited £4.7bn cited in the previous year.

Keith has collected over 500 signatures for the "reclaim VS.com" Scottish parliamentary petition campaign to bring the privately owned VisitScotland.com website, into public ownership. He added: "These figures suggest that the policy of increasing tourism in urban areas and expecting to trickle down is deeply flawed.

Scotland-wide, the January-June figures for "countryside areas" in both the B&B and hotel sectors showed zero growth year on year, while rising 2 per cent in each hospitality sector in the towns and cities.

Barbara Clark, a spokeswoman for VisitScotland, argued against seeing the figures as a reflection on the agency's marketing strategy: "It's not that simple. Figures go up and down depending on the provision in particular areas, which is why we don't use these as a measure of our success."

Rural Tourism Policy in Brazil

Rural tourism is still a segment that is under expansion in Brazil. This type of activity has been well known in the USA and Europe since the 1950s. It was only in the 80s, however, that it became a business activity in Brazil.

Rural tourism began when properties in Santa Catarina and in Rio Grande do Sul decided to diversify their activities to combat their financial difficulties by receiving tourists. This segment has since experienced gradual growth in Brazil, encouraged by the cultural regional diversity.

In the state of Amazonas, you can experience rural tourism in the jungle. In the state of Goiás, attractions include the waterfalls, lakes and geysers. In Minas Gerais, the local cheese, cachaça (rum) and friendly chats with locals are the attractions. In Mato Grosso do Sul you can ride a horse over the largest floodable area on the planet, while Espírito Santo is the cradle of agro-tourism. In the south, the tourist can experience the traditions and customs brought by European settlers.

According to a survey conducted by Embratur (Brazilian Tourism Company) in 2007, about 20% of foreigners who visit the country are interested in nature, ecotourism and adventure. Rural tourists will find activities such as fishing, adventure sports, hiking, visiting ranches and cultural houses, and recreational activities in the rural environment.

Green farms and rich flora and fauna each year attracts more tourists to Brazil.

The Ministry of Tourism is planning to use rural tourism to rescue and promote the cultural and natural heritage of the community. This segment also brings benefits to the local population with the improvement of their lives conditions, new job opportunities, and the reduction of rural-urban migration.

Tourism Policy of Germany

Tourism policy is an integral component of the German government's economic policy. The main principles, goals and instruments of Germany's tourism policy - both at the national level and in international forums - can be outlined as follows:

As in all economic sectors, the German government's central task in formulating and implementing its tourism policy is to boost entrepreneurial initiative and to enhance the competitiveness of tourism-related companies by continually fine-tuning the policy framework. This includes working together with the federal Länder and local governments to provide the necessary infrastructure for a successful tourism sector. In general, the Länder are responsible for the concrete planning, development and direct promotion of tourism.

The main economic policy areas through which the Federal Government has a formative influence on the tourism industry include tax policy, labour market policy and above all federal government policy on small and medium-sized businesses.

Government support measures that specifically benefit the tourism sector include federal funding for the German National Tourist Board and for projects to enhance the performance of the tourism industry.

The funding allocated to the German National Tourist Board is intended primarily to market Germany internationally as a holiday and travel destination. This type of marketing is necessary because - given the intensity of international competition - small-scale market participants in Germany are unable to perform this task entirely on their own. Funding for this purpose has steadily increased in recent years and amounted to approximately 26.3 million euros for the 2009 financial year.

Government funding to enhance the performance and competitiveness of the German tourism industry is used primarily to support advanced training programmes. This funding is also used to support projects that focus on market monitoring, quality enhancement for tourism products and services, and sales promotion. The primary aims here are to strengthen the performance of individual businesses and to foster environment-friendly practices in the tourism sector.

Another key goal is to provide targeted support for the marketing of innovative products and projects (such as tours for children and adolescents; environmentally compatible forms of travel; and accessible tourism). In these efforts, a particular priority is placed on meeting the needs of the new federal states in eastern Germany.

Furthermore, the Federal Government's rural development policy also includes support for rural tourism. This support forms a key component of the government's agricultural policy, and as such falls within the remit of the Federal Ministry of Food, Agriculture and Consumer Protection. Within the framework of the "Joint Task to Improve Agricultural Structures and Coastal Protection" (i.e. operated jointly by the Federal and Länder governments), the Agriculture Ministry and the Länder carry out measures to help rural businesses invest in agro-tourism and farm holidays, with the aim of diversifying rural income sources and strengthening rural economies.

Developing Rural Tourism in Finland Through Entrepreneurship

Rural tourism typically refers to tourism outside densely-populated areas and tourism centres. In some countries, the term 'farm tourism' is synonymous with rural tourism. Wilderness tourism and forest tourism can, in some contexts, be included in the concept of rural tourism, whereas in some other circumstances these terms can be considered as separate. In many countries, rural tourism is understood to be more or less synonymous with nature tourism or at least travelling in nature, and the 'framework' for rural tourism is usually offered by national parks and other publicly-owned land areas .

We examines the objectives of developing rural tourism from two different perspectives. Firstly, the development of rural tourism is examined in the context of Finnish rural-development policy. According to Siiskonen, rural policy is commonly seen as holistic, extensive development and it is described as coordinative and integrative. There is no established division between rural policy and rural development. Siiskonen (2002, p. 69), however, considers the strengthening of the economic activities and peoples' welfare in rural areas as the most-central objectives of this rural policy. The second perspective in this article relates to rural entrepreneurs. These two perspectives are considered because the former seeks to create conditions that influence the behaviour of the latter. By appreciating the dynamics of both aspects, there is greater likelihood of developing effective policy interventions.

Rural-Development Perspective

Rural tourism is often seen as one significant means of developing livelihoods particularly in areas with negative population growth. It is believed that rural tourism creates new jobs, decreases migration and helps to maintain the local level of services. According to international research, rural tourism also seems to particularly improve the position of women, as the majority of the tourism businesses in farms are family businesses. Equally, tourism has also increased local demand for primary-production businesses, particularly farm products, in rural areas. Rural-development strategy objectives generally aim towards the creation and maintenance of new jobs, the expansion of business activities, the support of public services and the creation of new free-time opportunities for travellers .

The development of rural tourism often specifically involves the economic and social development of a rural area. Rural tourism is a relatively small sector of the tourism industry from a global perspective, yet it still has great significance for local economies at many destinations. When the benefits yielded by tourism are generally examined in an area as gross income and person work years, many economic, social and environmental benefits with wider significance receive less attention. Tourism increases an awareness of, for example, a need for the preservation and development of local culture and can strengthen the local cultural identity. Many services, which also benefit the local population, stay alive with the help of tourism. The success of rural tourism is dependent on an attractive environment, which is why tourism often enhances the protection of nature and culture.

The rural-support programmes targeted inside and also outside the European Union have generated not only large-scale national, but also local rural-tourism development programmes. According to Clarke, Denman, Hickman, and Slovak (2001), the development of rural tourism is most successful when it is based on national strategy and co-ordination and strategy with local commitment and local actors. The success of tourism-development plans is dependent on both the administration's ability to support-development projects and the entrepreneurs' desire and ability to commit themselves to the development plans.

4 Rural Tourism Business

One of the ways that others around the world have done this is to develop tourism routes that create unique experiences for visitors (Australia, South Africa, Spain, France). Simply put - route tourism is "an initiative to bring together a variety of activities and attractions under a unified theme and thus stimulate entrepreneurial opportunity through the development of ancillary products and services". Routes link bundles of experiences for visitors and make it easier for them to make their way through the abundance of marketing information to a travel decision that satisfies their overall needs. One of favourite quotes on routes is that a" *route can be experienced without necessarily ever arriving at a destination, and in turn, a destination can be experienced without following a route"* (Murray and Graham, 1997).

Routes have emerged around the world primarily to link products in rural areas where awareness of products is enhanced by creating greater access for visitors who otherwise may not put in the effort to travel to an area. While the impacts of route tourism are still being studied, there is some evidence that routes promote partnership among tourism suppliers resulting in expanded market opportunities. Some have shown that visitors will stay longer and spend more in a region - something many rural areas are striving for.

This week I want to summarize some points from an article called "Route tourism: a roadmap for successful destinations and local economic development" written by Marlien Lourens. Marlien provides some good tips for those who were considering working on tourism routes based on evidence from South Africa and Spain case studies.

Step 1: The route must be grounded in solid market research that identifies key target markets and their needs - this must be done on an ongoing basis to be responsive to trends and shifts in markets.

Step 2: An audit should be done on the tourism products in the area including all natural and cultural assets. It may be valuable to determine criteria to be included as part of the route to ensure consistency of quality in the travel experience.

Step 3: Scrutinize the assets to determine the unique selling features of the area and then develop a macro level strategic plan to consolidate tourism planning for the area.

Step 4: Determine the size of the membership base for suppliers on the route - the buy in of these members is critical to the success of the route for they are the ultimate delivery agents of the experience. It is important to ensure the product mix is diverse and does not over represent any of the sectors (i.e. accommodations) as visitors will expect that all aspects of their experience will be available.

Step 5: Members should establish a clear brand identity for the route and then market this according to the targets identified.

Step 6: Members should decide upon what sort of governance and operational structure they need to ensure that the route is maintained.

Step 7: Members should think long term about the finances required to make the route a success in the minds of visitors. The author suggests that many routes start small and can take 20-30 years to mature and deliver substantial economic benefits and therefore realistic goals should be set about return on investment.

It might be worth considering the potential role of tourism routes to BC's product base as there are currently few well recognized routes available to visitors. While there are a few circle routes listed on the Tourism BC website and drivers see occasional signage on these routes when driving BC highways - there are questions about the level up uptake and ownership of these routes among BC operators or among residents.

Are these routes based on ongoing market research or random clusters of natural assets? Do people know about these routes? Are they uniquely positioned in the marketplace? Do operators know which routes they are on and do they tie into these to help position their products? These are all questions we need to ask to understand the impact of these routes or to develop new ones that tie together suppliers in ways that satisfy visitor's needs.

BUSINESS PLAN COMPETITION

The Inter-American Development Bank held a business plan competition for Caribbean tourism projects involving low-income communities in their value chains. The contest, organized by the IDB's Opportunities for the Majority Initiative, is open to companies based in the Bahamas, Barbados, Guyana, Haiti, Jamaica, Suriname and Trinidad and Tobago.

Eligible business plans included low-income communities as suppliers or distributors of goods or services, so that both companies and local residents benefit from the development of tourism ventures. Proposals will be judged on criteria such as innovations, economic, social and environmental impact on communities where projects would take place, growth potential, creditworthiness, implementation capacity and whether they could be replicated elsewhere.

The participants were required to submit a three-page summary of their project and a one-page outline of their company before April 9, 2010. IDB specialists will review the proposals and select up to ten entries for further development. The information was: "After taking part in a workshop, contestants will perfect their business plans for a final round of presentations to be held on July 23, 2010 before a panel of independent jurors."

Winning proposals will receive up to $25,000 in consulting services from internationally recognized firms specialized in tourism development, with the goal of preparing the business plans to become eligible for financing.

Opportunities for the Majority is a special IDB initiative that promotes and finances private-sector business models designed to deliver quality products and services, create employment, and enable low-income communities to join the formal economy in Latin America and the Caribbean.

How to Write a Tourism Business Plan

Having a business plan can help you achieve many things. For starters, you won't be able to obtain any type of credit or funding unless you have a business plan to present to the bank or financial institution. If you want to attract investors or partners, a business plan can help you establish how serious you are about the project and let them know what they can expect to gain if they join you.

1. Decide what type of business plan you want to write for your tourism business. If you are writing a business plan to help you get organized and understand the step-by-step process of setting up a business, you can skip certain details and avoid formal language. If you are writing a business plan in hopes of obtaining financial help or sponsorship, you will need a more thorough description of your plans.
2. Include all the basic financial details needed to convince a bank or lending institution that you know what you are doing. This includes a detailed description of your services, your marketing strategy, your projected income for the first year and your expenses for setting up the business, including permits.
3. Keep the business plan simple and understandable, but don't make it too short. Banks expect to see at least 20 pages of detailed information, including graphs and charts, but you can go on for as many as 40 pages if the information you have is important.

4. Consult with an expert to help you write your business plan. Unless you have the knowledge and ability to write well and convincingly, you may be better off paying a professional writer to work out a tourism business plan that is both comprehensive and interesting.
5. Visit BPlans.com to learn more about creating your own tourism business plan and to see dozens of samples of successful business plans . The website also offers video and audio tutorials to help you decide what type of business plan is better for your particular situation.

CHANGING SCENARIO

MALAYSIA is banking on the tourism sector this year as its number one money earner in terms of economic returns through the Asean Plus Three (Asean+3) pact with China, Korea and Japan.

East Asia Business Council (EABC) chairman Tan Sri Azman Hashim said efforts are underway to integrate single-owned hotels with other hotels overseas to create a platform for all the hotels to leverage on one another.

"We are very committed to promoting East Asia as we believe with Asean+3, we can achieve practical things much faster. We look forward to China, Japan and Korea helping us."

Azman was speaking at a press conference after launching the Ministry of International Trade and Industry symposium on expanding trade and investment linkages in East Asia themed "Business without Borders" in Kuala Lumpur yesterday.

The symposium was officiated by tMITI deputy minister Datuk Jacob Dungau Sagan. Chairman of the EABC tourism sub-committee, Datuk Syed Amin Al- Jeffri was also present.

Syed Amin said tourism remained one of the biggest money generators for Southeast Asian countries, with the industry worth nearly US$30-US$40 billion annually.

"The cooperation between Asean and the Asean+3 countries will create a regional tourism development strategy, strengthen regional links, raise quality of tourism products and services, and harmonise common interests of regional tourism as well as the interests of each Asean member country.

"We want to get China, Japan and Korea to form the East Asean Tourism Association and this is crucial in promoting tourism cooperation," he added.

Azman said the three East Asian countries are among the top 10 trading nations for Asean. The region's volume of trade with the three countries stood at USD413 billion or accounting for 27 per cent of Asean external trade in 2009.

ASEAN comprises Brunei, Cambodia, Indonesia, Laos, Malaysia, Myanmar, the Philippines, Singapore, Thailand and Vietnam.

A group of Chinese tourists lined up at a busy shopping district in downtown Seoul, chatting and laughing as their flag-waving guide hollered instructions just before they were to try their hand at making the famous Korean side dish kimchi.

Such a scene isn't out of the ordinary in this city - in fact, it's becoming all the more common as the number of tourists from the neighboring country visibly increases.

"We came here because of the Korean Wave," said Xiao Yongqiang, one of two Chinese guides leading the group of 17 tourists from Guangdong on China's southern coast. "We want to see, experience and buy everything that's in Korean dramas."

Some Chinese tourists have canceled trips to Japan and instead headed to Korea since a diplomatic row in September inflamed anti-Japanese sentiment in China.

"We have yet to receive statistics for September, but I heard tourism to Japan has dropped significantly," said Choi Hyo-jung, a publicity official at the China National Tourism Administration's branch in Seoul. "Korea may have surpassed Japan in terms of tourist arrivals from China."

The number of visitors from China has grown at a surprising pace in recent years - as much as 45 percent year-on-year during the January-August period - prompting Korea's tourism industry to shift its marketing focus from Japan to China.

Stores in shopping districts like Myeong-dong have added Chinese-speaking staff, their headquarters are using Korean celebrities popular across China and Southeast Asia in advertisements, and glitzy duty-free stores are dropping European luxury brands to give more space to Korean cosmetics chains that are less expensive but more popular in Asia.

Korea ranks among the top five destinations for outbound Chinese tourists, trailing only Hong Kong, Taiwan, Macau and Japan, according to statistics from the China National Tourism Administration.

Some 1.34 million tourists from China visited Korea last year, compared to 1.07 million in 2007 and 710,000 in 2005. The growth rate has been even steeper this year, with 1.26 million already counted as of August.

Visitors from China spend more than Japanese tourists while in Korea - $1,547 on average compared to $1,084, according to data from the official Korea Tourism Organization.

Small-sized stores are bracing for China's economic emergence.

The Seoul Chamber of Commerce, an association of businesses operating in the capital, opened a free Chinese language course in September for merchants working in Myeong-dong and Namdaemun and Dongdaemun markets, hoping to hone their communication skills.

China's growing profile has driven Korea to ease visa regulations for Chinese tourists and rush to resolve the shortage of accommodations.

"Most of our customers are still Japanese, but I've been noticing a visible increase in Chinese customers," said Kim Ye-sook, a proprietor of an eyeglass store at Namdaemun Market who was one of about 30 people attending the class, which is held three times a week. "I can see that the tide could change in three to four years, and I am preparing myself," she added. Yonhap

Environmentally Sound Rural Tourism Boosts Moroccan Economy

A Chemonics project is laying the groundwork for environmentally sound rural tourism development in Morocco, a country with a unique blend of Arab, Berber, and African cultural attractions.

Just a few weeks after the project's launch late last year, Chemonics put Morocco at center stage at the annual African travel industry's ecotourism conference in Fès, with keynote addresses by chief of party and leading ecotourism expert James MacGregor.

"An increasing number of travelers are interested in the rural tourism experience in Morocco," MacGregor said. "Our goal is to help Morocco capitalize on its rural tourism assets to further economic growth."

The six-day conference, sponsored by the Africa Travel Association, showcased Morocco's offerings to more than 150 U.S. tour operators, who sell tourism packages to American travelers.

Over the next three years, Chemonics will work with the Ministry of Tourism to create two dozen new tour itineraries in rural regions with the highest potential for tourism. The goal is to attract more U.S. and European tourists, helping to diversify the economy and create jobs.

Chemonics environmental and ecotourism specialist David Gibson, who also participated in the conference, presented case studies on fostering community participation in tourism product development, drawing on Chemonics' experience in Botswana, Madagascar, and Uganda.

"These successes have depended on participatory approaches that create partnerships between communities and tour operators—a key to infrastructure financing," he said. "Including rural communities in both the conception and development of tourism products is essential to guarantee sustainability."

From the imperial city of Fès to the famous beaches of Agadir, Morocco has plenty to offer international tourists. But despite its rich cultural and natural heritage, this North African country ranks only ninth among the 10 principal tourist destinations in the Mediterranean basin.

Morocco hopes to change that by boosting tourism in its small towns and villages — areas largely undiscovered by ecotourism, educational, and adventure travelers. Though a mere 5 percent of tourists to Morocco actually travel to rural areas, a visitor exit survey by Chemonics last year found that two out of three want more contact with rural communities.

To help meet this demand, the USAID-funded rural tourism development project focuses on institutional development, community-based tourism strategies, training, and the development of new and exciting tour products.

These efforts are expected to boost employment and incomes in rural areas, particularly as the United States and Morocco move closer to signing a Free Trade Agreement.

"Typically, free trade agreements have a significant impact on subsistence-level farms," said project supervisor Mohamed Khatouri. "Rural tourism, however, can play an important role in the transition from a traditional agricultural economy to the labor-intensive travel sector."

To facilitate the transition, Chemonics is working with tourism organizations, business associations, and regional tourism officials to promote effective, market-driven tourism strategies, products, and services.

"With the advent of the Free Trade Agreement, there is an urgency to create jobs," said MacGregor. "The biggest challenge will be to ensure that those associated with the new tours have the adequate training to offer quality products from the beginning."

Can The Arts Save Your Small Town?

Last weekend the author had one of those serendipitous happenings that keep his belief in magic alive. The topic of our monthly Revitalization Team meeting was to be art as an economic development tool. Who should appear at my info table at our small town summer festival but an expert in art towns!

Joe McArdle is a resident of Phoenixville, Pennsylvania, a former steel town that revitalized itself by attracting artists and selling itself as an art town. They've been at it for years with great success.

Here are some of Joe's sage suggestions:

1. Start Small to Grow Big

It's common these days for small towns to get excited about something and go for a big grant, or try to raise taxes to pay for something before thinking it through and doing the requisite planning.

Douglas County, Kansas is in an uproar about raising property taxes to pay for heritage enhancements to attract tourists.

Better to grow into something that to try to go big and fail.

2. Don't ask Left Brain People to do Right Brain Work

Artists are notoriously bad at marketing themselves. That's not always true, of course, but something that a community can offer, to help artists do what they do best – make art.

In Joe's home, Phoenixville, old vacant buildings were turned into arts incubators, with small low cost studio spaces created for working artists. The storefront is devoted to displaying their work.

Monthly art walks and arts events are put on by the town to attract potential buyers from nearby urban centers. Phoenixville was marketing itself as an art town.

3. Give Visitors a Reason Besides Art to Come to Your Town

Joe stressed that the best way to draw arts patrons, besides good art, is good food. Attracting good restaurants gives urbanites a reason to make your small town their getaway destination.

This is vastly oversimplified, but the core to Phoenixville's success is:

- Working slowly to build success.
- Nurturing artists by giving them great space and good marketing
- Giving visitors multiple reasons to plan a getaway to your art town – good food, good art, regular events and activities.

American Craftsman

The American Craftsman Style, or the American Arts and Crafts Movement, is an American domestic architectural, interior design, landscape design, applied arts, and the decorative arts style and lifestyle philosophy that began in the last years of the 19th century. As a comprehensive design and art movement it remained popular into the 1930s. However, in the decorative arts and architectural design it has continued with numerous revivals and restoration projects through present times.

The American Craftsman style has its origins from the British Arts and Crafts movement which began as a philosophy and artistic style founded by William Morris earlier in the 1860s. The British movement was a reaction to the Industrial Revolution, with its disregard for the individual worker and degradation of the dignity of human labor. Seeking to ennoble the craftsman once again, the movement emphasized the hand-made over the mass-produced.

The Arts and Crafts movement was also a reaction against the eclectic 'over-decorated' aesthetic of the Victorian era. It was an anti-Victorian movement, with William Morris a staunch socialist. However, the expensive fabrication and construction materials and costly hand-made techniques used meant that the created works of the movement were actually only serving a wealthy clientele, a seeming contradiction to its roots in the materialist dialectic and socialist philosophy. However the philosophy and aesthetics of the British Arts and Crafts movement inspired a wide variety of related but conceptually distinct design movements throughout Europe, as well as the 'American Craftsman' movement in North America.

UNITED STATES DEVELOPMENTS

While the British movement was a response to the Victorian, the Arts and Crafts style's arrival in the United States was precisely at the moment when the Victorian era was coming to a close. The American Arts and Crafts Movement did share the philosophy of the reform movement and encouraged originality, simplicity of form, local natural materials, and the visibility of handicraft. It was distinguished by being concerned with ennobling the modest homes of the rapidly expanding American middle class, which became the Craftsman Bungalow style.

In the late 1890s, a group of Boston's more influential architects, designers, and educators were determined to bring the design reforms begun in Britain by William Morris to America. Their first meeting, to organize an exhibition of contemporary craft objects, was held in January 1897 at the Museum of Fine Arts, Boston (MFA). Present at this meeting were local: museum trustees including General Charles Loring, William Sturgis Bigelow, and Denman Ross; art collectors and patrons; writers and art critics, such as Sylvester Baxter for the *Boston Evening Transcript*; and artists and architects, such as Ross Turner and Ralph Clipson Sturgis.

They succeeded in opening the first American Arts and Crafts Exhibition in April 1897 at Copley Hall, featuring over 1000 objects made by 160 craftsmen, half of whom were craftswomen. Some of the exhibit's supporters included: the founder of Harvard's School of Architecture Langford Warren; social reformers Mrs. Richard Morris Hunt; Arthur Astor Carey and Edwin Mead; and graphic designer Will Bradley. When consumers and manufacturers realized the aesthetic and technical potential of the Arts and Crafts style's applied arts, the process with craftsmen and designers for design reform in Boston commenced.

Society of Arts and Crafts

The exhibition's success brought the formation of The Society of Arts and Crafts in June 1897, with a mandate to "Develop and encourage higher standards in the handicrafts." The twenty one founders, including Charles Elliot Norton, focused beyond consumer sales marketing, focusing on the relationship of artists and designers to the world of commerce, encouraging them to produce work with workmanship and design of the highest qualities.

The Society of Arts and Crafts mandate was soon expanded into a credo which read:

This Society was incorporated for the purpose of promoting artistic work in all branches of handicraft. It hopes to bring Designers and Workmen into mutually helpful relations, and to encourage workmen to execute designs of their own. It endeavors to stimulate in workmen an appreciation of the dignity and value of good design; to counteract the popular impatience of Law and Form, and the desire for over-ornamentation and specious originality. It will insist upon the necessity of sobriety and restraint, or ordered arrangement, of due regard for the relation between the form of an object and its use, and of harmony and fitness in the decoration put upon it.

The Craftsman

In the United States the Arts and Crafts style incorporated locally handcrafted wood, glass, and metal work creating objects that were both simple and elegant. In architecture, reacting to both Victorian architectural opulence and increasingly common mass-produced housing, the style incorporated a visible sturdy structure, of clean lines and natural materials. The movement's name American Craftsman came from the popular magazine, "The Craftsman," founded in 1901 by philosopher, designer, furniture maker, and editor Gustav Stickley. The magazine featured original house and furniture designs by Harvey Ellis, the Greene and Greene company, and others. The designs, while influenced by the ideals of the British movement, found inspiration in specifically American antecedents such as Shaker furniture and the Mission Revival Style, and the Anglo-Japanese style. Emphasis on the originality of the artist/craftsman led to the later design concepts of the 1930s Art Deco movement.

CRAFTSMAN ARCHITECTURAL DESIGN

Several developments in the American domestic architecture of the period are traceable not only to changes in taste and style but also to the shift from the upper- to middle-class patronage. The American Victorian typically took the form of a two-story square house with a hip roof disguised behind a variety of two-storied bays, with an assortment of gables as well as octagonal or round turrets and wraparound porches presenting a complex facade.

Typically, the basic square house was also complemented by a back wing complete with its own entrances, and a stairwell that housed the kitchen, pantries, and scullery on the first floor and the servants' quarters on the second. Fitted with inferior-quality woodwork and hardware, and noticeably smaller bedrooms and lower ceiling heights, the Victorian kitchen-servants' wing embodied the aristocratic class distinctions of the Old World.

With the large bays, turrets, and rear wing removed, the front porch simplified, and the ceilings lowered somewhat, it is not difficult to see how the American Foursquare developed from the common American Queen Anne. The middle-class housewife of the era would not have domestic servants (at least not live-in ones) and would be doing much if not all of the housework herself, as well as watching the children. These added roles made it important that the kitchen be integrated into the main house with easy sight lines to the common areas of the main floor (the dining and living rooms) as well as to the back yard. Commonly, the butler's pantry of the Victorian Era was replaced with dining room cabinetry that often consisted of "built-ins", which gave home designers the opportunity to incorporate wood and glass craftsmanship into the public aspects of the home.

Another common design development arising from the class-shift of the time was the built-in "breakfast nook" in the kitchen. The Victorian kitchen of the previous era was separated from the family view and daily routine. It typically had a work table (having the equivalent purpose of the modern countertop) at which the servants would eat after the family meal was served and the kitchen tidied.

The Victorian kitchen had no "proper" place for a family member to sit, eat, or do anything else. Again, as the housewife of the Craftsman era was now preparing the family meals, the Victorian kitchen gave way to one designed as the heart of the family's daily life. The breakfast nook often placed under a window or in its own bay provided a place for the family to gather at any time of the day or evening, particularly while food was being prepared.

Craftsman Architects

In Southern California the firm Greene and Greene are the most renowned practitioners of the original American Craftsman Style, and were based in Pasadena, California. Their projects for Ultimate bungalows include the Gamble House and Robert R. Blacker House in Pasadena, and the Thorsen House in Berkeley - with numerous others in California. Other examples in the Los Angeles region include the Lummis House

In Northern California the architects Bernard Maybeck, with the Swedenborgian Church (San Francisco, California); and Julia Morgan, with the Asilomar Conference Grounds and Mills College projects, are renowned for their well planned and detailed projects in the Craftsman style. Many other designers and projects represent the style in the region.

In San Diego, California the style was also popular. Architect David Owen Dryden designed and built many Craftsman California bungalows in the North Park district, now a proposed Dryden Historic District. The 1905 Marston House of George Marston in Balboa Park was designed by local architects Irving Gill and William Hebbard.

Frank Lloyd Wright, one of the most important and prolific architects of houses in the U.S., was one of the originators of the Prairie School style, which was an organic architecture outgrowth of both the American Craftsman style aesthetics and its philosophy for quality middle-class home design. Wright's career spanned through the Victorian, Chicago School, American Craftsman, Prairie School, International style, and Modernism movements. The Robie House is an example of his American Craftsman inspired Prairie School work.

In the early 1900s, developer Herberg J. Hapgood built numbers of Craftsman-style homes, many from stucco, that comprise the lakeside borough of Mountain Lakes, New Jersey. Residents were called "Lakers," though Hapgood eventually went bankrupt. The homes followed signature styles, including bungalows and chalets.

5 Rural Tourism Environment

Living in a remote location such as a rural area can have its advantages as well as its disadvantages. One of the more obvious advantages would be privacy. In many rural communities neighbors are fewer and far between than they are in the suburban areas, allowing more freedom to the occupants.

Living in a remote location such as a rural area can have its advantages as well as its disadvantages. One of the more obvious advantages would be privacy. In many rural communities neighbors are fewer and far between than they are in the suburban areas, allowing more freedom to the occupants.

Building codes are more relaxed as well. Pets and animals can be kept and gardening, a popular pastime in rural areas, becomes more practical. Gardening can serve more than just a hobbyist's pastime. It can serve to offset the costs of produce, and assist in a steady food surplus for the rural family.

A few of the disadvantages include increased time commuting to and from work, increased power outages and more difficulty accessing high speed internet and cable television. Of the people who choose to live in rural areas they agree that the disadvantages for them outweigh the disadvantages of living in more remote locations.

In many instances the differences between rural dwellers and urban residents are quite vast. They do not often cross lines such as urban dwellers to move to the country, or for rural dwellers to enter successfully into urban life or embrace urban culture and lifestyles.

There is no right or wrong way to live, be it either rural life, or urban living. The two are just so vastly and culturally adverse that not often are lines crossed successfully. People who move from urban areas into rural areas often find the lifestyle too relaxed, and lose patience easily, people who move from the more relaxed life of rural life often times find it difficult to adapt to the faster paced lifestyle.

Though some people do make the transition with varying levels of success, most people find the change to difficult to adapt to. There are a number of reasons one might attempt such a life altering cultural change including but not limited to health reasons, levels of stress, relationship issues, and mid life crisis in which a person feels they need an abrupt and very drastic change in their lifestyles to feel young again.

There is no real surprise why some people feel this need for such a drastic change. Our society according to some leading analysts and psychologists has changed from a progressive society based on domestic harmony into that of a short sixty second society. They begin to feel that something is missing in their lives, and reach out to the simple country life for a change in pace.

CLOSE TO NATURE

Folks have probably heard about a new type of getaway called the "staycation". A staycation is a vacation one takes close to home, to enjoy the adventures in their own backyard.

Why are staycations growing in popularity? There are many reasons for this trend including:

1. We have a "been there, done that" generation that has travelled far more than any other generation before it. It is no longer unique to travel to Europe, Southeast Asia or Africa because so many others have done this. In tourism we call this phenomenon "mass follows class" which

means that while a few intrepid tourists find unique places, they soon share their experiences leading to the flow of mass travellers after them. Tourism is an activity with incredible "social bragging rights", and these rights go up when others are less likely to have gone where you have travelled. So how does this lead to a staycation? Staycations are somewhat less common than they used to be and people are now more prone to explore what is in their own backyard.

2. Concerns about the carbon footprint of travel are also making people rethink international travel. While all travel produces carbon, air travel is becoming more scrutinized for its contribution to global warming. And beyond air travel, people are looking to invest in travel experiences that benefit places and people.
3. The experience of travel to and from destinations is becoming a hassle for many. Increased security measures, confusion about regulations, required passports, screening practices and add on taxes are common complaints of air travelers. These hassles are felt more so by people who have to travel for their work and leads many to want to avoid travel when they have leisure time.
4. The pace of society in both work and leisure time has created a need for people to "slow down". Many have tried to create space to be more slow by packing less into their schedule - including travel experiences.

As people look to stay closer to home for their vacations, rural areas that are developing tourism stand to benefit. In order to benefit however, rural areas need to become more visible to urbanites. This is not an easy task as many Canadians are becoming increasingly disconnected to the rural landscape and the amenities, communities and people within. At your next social gathering when someone asks you where you are going on your summer vacation - suggest some rural areas in your province and see if they know where you are talking about. I have done this often when I tell folks that I'd like to get to the Chilcotin this summer... I can see their blank stares that indicate they have no clue where I am talking about.

For those working in rural tourism - you may want to ask yourself if your area could be attractive to urbanites who want to staycation this year. What do you have that could help them slow down, stay close to home and explore, reduce their carbon footprint and experience reality in their own life? Chances are, there are many things that would suit staycationers.

Now how can you raise awareness that your rural area is worth exploring? Work with other small communities in your region and think about targeting some promotions to nearby urban markets. Assemble some packages that leave room for lots of exploration and flexibility while making it easy for them to decide.

And start a buzz about staycations within the industry to encourage organizations to work together to market BC to British Columbians, spur the rubber tire market and revitalize rural tourism efforts. The spin offs?

Rural areas will see increased visitation, added exposure may lead some people to relocate to rural areas as residents or to start a new business and BC residents will become better ambassadors for the province because they will know about its amenities (and will pass it on to other visitors).

Dark Side

Rural areas experience a number of environmental problems like pollutions of air, water and land, land degradation and urbanization.

Air Pollution in villages is caused due to burning of agricultural wastes and straw, burning of fire wood and dung cakes, and decomposition of crop wastes and animal wastes. Considerable amount of methane produced due to bio-degradation of crop residues and animal wastes contribute heavily in the rural air pollution. Rural ladies suffer from many respiratory and eye diseases as they cook food by burning wood. Rural houses are often built unscientifically.

Due to this the extent of indoor air pollution is greater in these areas. The practice of Jhoom- cultivation damages forests and other vegetations on one hand and enhances the CO_2 load on the atmosphere on the other hand. The increasing concentration of CO_2 in the atmosphere contributes to the Global Warming.

Principal water pollutants in the rural areas are animal wastes and agrochemicals like synthetic fertilizers, pesticides, hormones etc. These chemicals reach to the water bodies of the rural areas through surface run off where they cause Eutrophication. Eutrophication is the nutrient enrichment of water bodies. In Eutrophication, varieties of aquatic plants grow in the water that absorbs dissolved oxygen. The scarcity of dissolved oxygen in the water kills aquatic animals and plants. The bacteria that go to decompose those bodies further absorb the oxygen causing its acute scarcity and the process goes on.

Pesticides are poisonous chemicals that are applied in agriculture to kill pests. These chemicals join water bodies through the surface run off, enter into the food-chains and get accumulated inside fruits, grains and vegetables and bodies of aquatic animals. This is called as bio-accumulation. Biologically accumulated poisons in the animal bodies go on increasing and this process is called as Bio-magnification. Pesticides accumulate and get magnified into the fatty tissues of human beings through fish and other aquatic foods.

Land pollution in rural areas is caused due to dumping of animal wastes, agricultural residues and mixing of agrochemicals in the soil.Animal wastes dumped on the ground, leach into the soil and contaminate water sources. Secondly, these wastes invite a number of parasitic worms & disease causing micro organisms to develop and spread in the environment through water and air. These worms and micro organisms cause various types of diseases in rural people. Decomposing residues of agricultural materials produce lots of methane and encourage the production of disease causing micro organisms. Agrochemicals like synthetic fertilizers alter the composition of soil and make it infertile. Pesticides applied in fields kill soil micro organisms and enter into the food chain and reach to human beings. Bio- accumulations of poisonous pesticides in human beings cause diseases of nervous system, kidneys and reproductive systems in human beings.

Pesticides laced seeds are often eaten by birds that visit fields frequently. Thus different types of seed eating birds are vanishing out of rural areas. Such incidents have been reported from Rajasthan, an Indian state where many peacocks died after eating pesticide laced seeds. The population of sparrows is vanishing out of many Indian states due to application of pesticides on large scale.

Since the days of green revolution, Mono agriculture has been encouraged to raise production of crops on commercial level. Mono agriculture is the practice of growing single crop on a large farm repeatedly for many years. This practice demands more care, more fertilizers and more pesticides.

When topmost fertile layer of soil is washed away through rain water or it is carried away by wind, the process is called as soil erosion. Thus wind and rainfall are the principal factors that cause soil erosion.

Soil erosion is the major problem of rural environment. It is caused due to-

(i) Overgrazing by cattle.

(ii) Deforestation and denudation of land.

(iii) Cultivation along river banks.

Over grazing is the activity of repeated grazing by cattle including sheep and goats, in a particular field. This results into the complete loss of grass species leaving the land uncovered. Such a land becomes prone to soil erosion through rain –water and by wind. The human activity of cutting forest trees puts severe stress on land and atmosphere. A land denuded of forests and other vegetation, is always prone to serious soil erosion.

Loss of forests makes numerous species of birds and animals homeless and causes adverse alterations in climatic conditions. Cultivation along river banks makes the soil loose. Loose soil can easily be washed away into the river during rains. Most of the Indian rivers have been silted severely due to heavy soil erosions in the catchments areas. This condition is the root cause of floods in different Indian states during rainy seasons.

Natural Environment

The natural environment, encompasses all living and non-living things occurring naturally on Earth or some region thereof. It is an environment that encompasses the interaction of all living species.

The natural environment is contrasted with the built environment, which comprises the areas and components that are strongly influenced by humans. A geographical area is regarded as a natural environment, if the human impact on it is kept under a certain limited level.

Earth science generally recognizes four spheres, the lithosphere, the hydrosphere, the atmosphere, and the biosphere as correspondent to rocks, water, air, and life. Some scientists include, as part of the spheres of the Earth, the cryosphere (corresponding to ice) as a distinct portion of the hydrosphere, as well as the pedosphere (corresponding to soil) as an active and intermixed sphere.

Earth science is an all-embracing term for the sciences related to the planet Earth. There are four major disciplines in earth sciences, namely geography, geology, geophysics and geodesy. These major disciplines use physics, chemistry, biology, chronology and mathematics to build a qualitative and quantitative understanding of the principal areas or *spheres* of the Earth system.

An ocean is a major body of saline water, and a component of the hydrosphere. Approximately 71% of the Earth's surface (an area of some 362 million square kilometers) is covered by ocean, a continuous body of water that is customarily divided into several principal oceans and smaller seas. More than half of this area is over 3,000 meters (9,800 ft) deep. Average oceanic salinity is around 35 parts per thousand (ppt) (3.5%), and nearly all seawater has a salinity in the range of 30 to 38 ppt.

Though generally recognized as several 'separate' oceans, these waters comprise one global, interconnected body of salt water often referred to as the World Ocean or global ocean. This concept of a global ocean as a continuous body of water with relatively free interchange among its parts is of fundamental importance to oceanography. The major oceanic divisions are defined in part by the continents, various archipelagos, and other criteria: these divisions are (in descending order of size) the Pacific Ocean, the Atlantic Ocean, the Indian Ocean, the Southern Ocean and the Arctic Ocean.

Rivers

A river is a natural watercourse, usually freshwater, flowing toward an ocean, a lake, a sea or another river. In a few cases, a river simply flows into the ground or dries up completely before reaching another body of water. Small rivers may also be termed by several other names, including stream, creek and brook. In the United States a river is generally classified as a watercourse more than 60 feet (18 metres) wide.

The water in a river is usually in a channel, made up of a stream bed between banks. In larger rivers there is also a wider floodplain shaped by flood-waters over-topping the channel. Flood plains may be very wide in relation to the size of the river channel. Rivers are a part of the hydrological cycle. Water within a river is generally collected from precipitation through surface runoff, groundwater recharge, springs, and the release of water stored in glaciers and snowpacks.

Streams

A stream is a flowing body of water with a current, confined within a bed and stream banks. Streams play an important corridor role in connecting fragmented habitats and thus in conserving biodiversity. The study of streams and waterways in general is known as *surface hydrology.* Types of streams include creeks, tributaries, which do not reach an ocean and connect with another stream or river, brooks, which are typically small streams and sometimes sourced from a spring or seep and tidal inlets.

Lakes

Natural lakes on Earth are generally found in mountainous areas, rift zones, and areas with ongoing or recent glaciation. Other lakes are found in endorheic basins or along the courses of mature rivers. In some parts of the world, there are many lakes because of chaotic drainage patterns left over from the last Ice Age. All lakes are temporary over geologic time scales, as they will slowly fill in with sediments or spill out of the basin containing them.

Ponds

A pond is a body of standing water, either natural or man-made, that is usually smaller than a lake. A wide variety of man-made bodies of water are classified as ponds, including water gardens designed for aesthetic ornamentation, fish ponds designed for commercial fish breeding, and solar ponds designed to store thermal energy. Ponds and lakes are distinguished from streams via current speed. While currents in streams are easily observed, ponds and lakes possess thermally driven micro-currents and moderate wind driven currents. These features distinguish a pond from many other aquatic terrain features, such as stream pools and tide pools.

ATMOSPHERE, CLIMATE AND WEATHER

The atmosphere of the Earth serves as a key factor in sustaining the planetary ecosystem. The thin layer of gases that envelops the Earth is held in place by the planet's gravity. Dry air consists of 78% nitrogen, 21% oxygen, 1% argon and other inert gases, such as carbon dioxide. The remaining gases are often referred to as trace gases, among which are the greenhouse gases such as water vapor, carbon dioxide, methane, nitrous oxide, and ozone. Filtered air includes trace amounts of many other chemical compounds.

Air also contains a variable amount of water vapor and suspensions of water droplets and ice crystals seen as clouds. Many natural substances may be present in tiny amounts in an unfiltered air sample, including dust, pollen and spores, sea spray, volcanic ash, and meteoroids. Various industrial pollutants also may be present, such as chlorine (elementary or in compounds), fluorine compounds, elemental mercury, and sulphur compounds such as sulphur dioxide [SO_2].

The ozone layer of the Earth's atmosphere plays an important role in depleting the amount of ultraviolet (UV) radiation that reaches the surface. As DNA is readily damaged by UV light, this serves to protect life at the surface. The atmosphere also retains heat during the night, thereby reducing the daily temperature extremes.

Effects of Global Warming

The potential dangers of global warming are being increasingly studied by a wide global consortium of scientists. These scientists are increasingly concerned about the potential long-term effects of global warming on our natural environment and on the planet. Of particular concern is how climate change and global warming caused by anthropogenic, or human-made releases of greenhouse gases, most notably carbon dioxide, can act interactively, and have adverse effects upon the planet, its natural environment and humans' existence.

Efforts have been increasingly focused on the mitigation of greenhouse gases that are causing climatic changes, on developing adaptative strategies to global warming, to assist humans, animal and plant species, ecosystems, regions and nations in adjusting to the effects of global warming. Some examples of recent collaboration to address climate change and global warming include:

Another view of the Aletsch Glacier in the Swiss Alps and because of global warming it has been decreasing

- The United Nations Framework Convention Treaty and convention on Climate Change, to stabilize greenhouse gas concentrations in the atmosphere at a level that would prevent dangerous anthropogenic interference with the climate system.
- The Kyoto Protocol, which is the protocol to the international Framework Convention on Climate Change treaty, again with the objective of reducing greenhouse gases in an effort to prevent anthropogenic climate change.
- The Western Climate Initiative, to identify, evaluate, and implement collective and cooperative ways to reduce greenhouse gases in the region, focusing on a market-based cap-and-trade system.

A significantly profound challenge is to identify the natural environmental dynamics in contrast to environmental changes not within natural variances. A common solution is to adapt a static view neglecting natural variances to exist. Methodologically, this view could be defended when looking at processes which change slowly and short time series, while the problem arrives when fast processes turns essential in the object of the study.

Climate

Climate encompasses the statistics of temperature, humidity, atmospheric pressure, wind, rainfall, atmospheric particle count and numerous other meteorological elements in a given region over long periods of time. Climate can be contrasted to weather, which is the present condition of these same elements over periods up to two weeks.

The climate of a location is affected by its latitude, terrain, altitude, ice or snow cover, as well as nearby water bodies and their currents. Climates can be classified according to the average and typical ranges of different variables, most commonly temperature and precipitation. The most commonly used classification scheme is the one originally developed by Wladimir Köppen. The Thornthwaite system, in use since 1948, incorporates evapotranspiration in addition to temperature and precipitation information and is used in studying animal species diversity and potential impacts of climate changes. The Bergeron and Spatial Synoptic Classification systems focus on the origin of air masses defining the climate for certain areas.

Weather

Weather is a set of all the phenomena occurring in a given atmospheric area at a given time. Most weather phenomena occur in the troposphere, just below the stratosphere. Weather refers, generally, to day-to-day temperature and precipitation activity, whereas climate is the term for the average atmospheric conditions over longer periods of time. When used without qualification, "weather" is understood to be the weather of Earth.

Weather occurs due to density (temperature and moisture) differences between one place and another. These differences can occur due to the sun angle at any particular spot, which varies by latitude from the tropics.

The strong temperature contrast between polar and tropical air gives rise to the jet stream. Weather systems in the mid-latitudes, such as extratropical cyclones, are caused by instabilities of the jet stream flow. Because the Earth's axis is tilted relative to its orbital plane, sunlight is incident at different angles at different times of the year. On the Earth's surface, temperatures usually range ±40 °C (100 °F to "40 °F) annually. Over thousands of years, changes in the Earth's orbit have affected the amount and distribution of solar energy received by the Earth and influence long-term climate

Surface temperature differences in turn cause pressure differences. Higher altitudes are cooler than lower altitudes due to differences in compressional heating. Weather forecasting is the application of science and technology to predict the state of the atmosphere for a future time and a given location. The atmosphere is a chaotic system, and small changes to one part of the system can grow to have large effects on the system as a whole. Human attempts to control the weather have occurred throughout human history, and there is evidence that human activity such as agriculture and industry has inadvertently modified weather patterns.

Evidence suggests that life on Earth has existed for about 3.7 billion years. All known life forms share fundamental molecular mechanisms, and based on these observations, theories on the origin of life attempt to find a mechanism explaining the formation of a primordial single cell organism from which all life originates. There are many different hypotheses regarding the path that might have been taken from simple organic molecules via pre-cellular life to protocells and metabolism.

Although there is no universal agreement on the definition of life, scientists generally accept that the biological manifestation of life is characterized by organization, metabolism, growth, adaptation, response to stimuli and reproduction. Life may also be said to be simply the characteristic state of organisms. In biology, the science of living organisms, "life" is the condition which distinguishes active organisms from inorganic matter, including the capacity for growth, functional activity and the continual change preceding death.

A diverse array of living organisms (life forms) can be found in the biosphere on Earth, and properties common to these organisms—plants, animals, fungi, protists, archaea, and bacteria—are a carbon- and water-based cellular form with complex organization and heritable genetic information. Living organisms undergo metabolism, maintain homeostasis, possess a capacity to grow, respond to stimuli, reproduce and, through natural selection, adapt to their environment in successive generations. More complex living organisms can communicate through various means.

ECOSYSTEMS

An ecosystem(also called as environment) is a natural unit consisting of all plants, animals and micro-organisms (biotic factors) in an area functioning together with all of the non-living physical (abiotic) factors of the environment.

Central to the ecosystem concept is the idea that living organisms are continually engaged in a highly interrelated set of relationships with every other element constituting the environment in which they exist. Eugene Odum, one of the founders of the science of ecology, stated: "Any unit that includes all of the organisms (ie: the "community") in a given area interacting with the physical environment so that a flow of energy leads to clearly defined trophic structure, biotic diversity, and material cycles (i.e.: exchange of materials between living and nonliving parts) within the system is an ecosystem."

The human ecosystem concept is then grounded in the deconstruction of the human/nature dichotomy, and the emergent premise that all species are ecologically integrated with each other, as well as with the abiotic constituents of their biotope. A greater number or variety of species or biological diversity of an ecosystem may contribute to greater resilience of an ecosystem, because there are more species present at a location to respond to change and thus "absorb" or reduce its effects. This reduces the effect before the ecosystem's structure is fundamentally changed to a different state. This is not universally the case and there is no proven relationship between the species diversity of an ecosystem and its ability to provide goods and services on a sustainable level.

Humid tropical forests produce very few goods and direct services and are extremely vulnerable to change, while many temperate forests readily grow back to their previous state of development within a lifetime after felling or a forest fire. Some grasslands have been sustainably exploited for thousands of years (Mongolia, European peat and moorland communities).

The term ecosystem can also pertain to human-made environments, such as human ecosystems and human-influenced ecosystems, and can describe any situation where there is relationship between living organisms and their environment. Fewer areas on the surface of the earth today exist free from human contact, although some genuine wilderness areas continue to exist without any forms of human intervention.

BIOMES

Biomes are terminologically similar to the concept of ecosystems, and are climatically and geographically defined areas of ecologically similar climatic conditions on the Earth, such as communities of plants, animals, and soil organisms, often referred to *as* ecosystems. Biomes are defined on the basis of factors such as plant structures (such as trees, shrubs, and grasses), leaf types (such as broadleaf and needleleaf), plant spacing (forest, woodland, savanna), and climate. Unlike ecozones, biomes are not defined by genetic, taxonomic, or historical similarities. Biomes are often identified with particular patterns of ecological succession and climax vegetation.

Wilderness is generally defined as a natural environment on Earth that has not been significantly modified by human activity. The WILD Foundation goes into more detail, defining wilderness as: "The most intact, undisturbed wild natural areas left on our planet - those last truly wild places that humans do not control and have not developed with roads, pipelines or other industrial infrastructure." Wilderness areas and protected parks are considered important for the survival of certain species, ecological studies, conservation, solitude, and recreation. Wilderness is deeply valued for cultural, spiritual, moral, and aesthetic reasons. Some nature writers believe wilderness areas are vital for the human spirit and creativity.

Wildlife includes all non-domesticated plants, animals and other organisms. Domesticating wild plant and animal species for human benefit has occurred many times all over the planet, and has a major impact on the environment, both positive and negative. Wildlife can be found in all ecosystems. Deserts, rain forests, plains, and other areas—including the most developed urban sites—all have distinct forms of wildlife. While the term in popular culture usually refers to animals that are untouched by human factors, most scientists agree that wildlife around the world is impacted by human activities.

6 DEVELOPMENT OF RURAL TOURISM

With the rapid development of the socioeconomic life of the public and the increasing work pressure. City people have gradually tired of the city's fast-paced atmosphere of life, eager to seek back to nature feel, while the rural tourism is to meet the needs of these visitors has gradually become a tourist hot spot in the new century. This chapter analyzes the rural tourism development on the new rural construction mechanism, analyzes the status of Wulong rural tourism development and issues on how to develop rural tourism Wulong made a number of countermeasures and suggestions.

As competition intensifies, the city people's work life, increasing pressure on, eager to return to nature, relax body and mind. The natural, fresh and pastoral scenery and rich Culture of rural folk characteristics of rural tourism, sightseeing tours abroad, compared with the save time, money advantage, is to meet the needs of the public in recent years has developed very rapidly, prospects are bright.

We believe that the concept of rural tourism has two aspects: First place in rural areas; second is a rural nature as a tourist attraction, the two are indispensable. In summary, the basic identity "refers to rural village tourism is a unique natural environment, rural scenery, production and management patterns, folk customs, farming culture, and rural settlements other resources, to provide for tourists sightseeing, leisure, vacation, experience, fitness, entertainment and shopping of a new type of tourism activities.

Rural Tourism and its core is a community rural tourism, rural tourism occurs in rural areas provided by the rural environment, rural heritage, rural life and rural activities. Rural Tourism and new rural construction promote each other and affect each other.

Party Plenum proposed "the development of production and living off the village Yung clean, rural air civilized, and democratic management" the task of building new socialist countryside, rural tourism development relies on the majority of resource distribution in rural areas to agricultural production , the villagers living in rural style, folk Culture as the main content is a casual agricultural production and tourism as one of the agricultural production business model. Rural Tourism and the new countryside construction of a high degree of internal unity, rural tourism can stimulate new countryside construction, the new rural construction can also promote rural tourism development .

Rural tourism association and strong and can effectively adjust the industrial structure, promoting the development of production Significant correlation of the tourism industry, according to estimates, tourism industry-related industries on the pull ratio of 1:4, as a follow-up of traditional agriculture industry, rural tourism development can be extended supply chain of agricultural products to effectively promote local agricultural products and hand - handicraft processing, food service, transportation, real estate and commercial and trade-related industries, not only can effectively promote the rural surplus labor force to secondary and tertiary industries of the transfer, optimizing the industrial structure, to achieve "production development" and promote in rural areas, economic and productive development.

Villager involved in tourism services to increase income and achieve poverty alleviation Growth in peasant incomes the key to the building of new socialist countryside. Direct benefit of the development of rural tourism is to create employment opportunities, increase their income. Farmers can by to work, shop, native products processing and Marketing to increase revenue, also available through tourism projects shareholder dividend income;

to tour to support farming, in order to promote agricultural tours, farm tour unity. At the same time to increase the income of the farmers to fully absorb the idle labor purposes.

Travel demand-driven improvement of the environment in rural areas, The tourism Industry has strong domestic demand, the driving force of the various elements of the tourism industry (food, shelter, transportation, travel, shopping, entertainment) on rural tourism services and reception facilities and set higher requirements. In order to adapt to tourism development, access to more economic benefits, the villagers would consciously to improve the internal environment (living environment, tourism, service level, etc.), and the external environment (cleanliness degree of the village, local landscape shaping, etc.), the villagers of the environment to strengthen the awareness of the village cleanliness degree of tolerance can be improved.

In the tourism demonstration effect, it can be a more general increase in the quality of the local Population . The tourism industry is relatively low barriers to entry, in carrying out rural tourism areas, service principal is the local residents. By developing the tourism industry, to carry out accommodation, catering, entertainment, travel services, breaking the relatively closed nature of country living space, you can broaden their horizons and accept new things. Driven by economic benefits, the villagers are willing to learn new knowledge and acquire new skills, so that the villagers, culture and civilization level is improved.

To promote rural tourism, construction and management of grass-roots democracy concept of update . The development of rural tourism in rural areas can promote the building of the system, ideas, updates and management of the democratization. Under the concept of modern enterprise system, the tourism regulatory body in the running, you can effectively affect the practitioners of the legal concept, moral values, democratic values and so on, the villagers rely on the management and introduced into a democratization of the practical problems in order to solve their own field of vision, the other regions can provide Experience of democracy. Wulong county Development of Rural Tourism Wulong County, rural tourism resources and tourism products are very rich in mountains and clouds, trees, farms orchards patchwork, climate cool and pleasant, natural scenery unique, a good ecological environment. Wulong is a tourist county, with Furong, world natural heritage, such as natural Bridge, Xiannushan AAAA-class tourist zone countries such as brands such as tourism products as their support.

In recent years, Wulong County, relying on its own unique natural and cultural resources, and actively promote agricultural tourism, leisure and holiday tourism, rural tourism emerged in the ascendant makes a good momentum of development.

Wulong County Rural Tourism Development focuses mainly on four characteristics: First, for a "green corridor" and "Green Home" and "Green base" construction, start Xiannushan leisure area, kiwi fruit production base for sightseeing park, "Baicao Garden", "100 Orchard," and so on eco-projects, in order to Wulong County, adds a new rural tourist resources and products. Second, feature rich rural tourism products. Wulong county rich in tofu, crystalline silk powder Shao, Claw Laocu, snow Jin tea and so on, has "township of Chinese dried bean curd," said. Third, the rural tourism industry to flourish.

"Nongjiale" the rise of tourism projects to promote rural tourism in the further development of the county, has taken shape in order to farm grill (lamb, grilled chicken, grilled fish, etc.), rather farm characteristics of Chinese food snacks (soil eggs, Jue base powder, the old meat, bamboo shoots, Shao powder, potatoes flowers, red Shao rice porridge, fresh vegetables, etc.), buffet; exclusive outdoor tent to sleep, mountain horse racing, jungle adventure tourist attractions, as represented by industry groups in order to Fairy Mountain Tour food and features a combination of agriculture and tourism products of eco-tourism development pattern is taking shape.

Fourth, to promote rural tourism brand to be. Chongqing through the organization of the first section of forest tourism, ecological landscape photography festival, Wulong Wu River Culture Festival, Wulong Tujia Ethnic plot, Treats drifting ferry festival festivals and other large activities, Wulong County, rural tourism has reached a certain reputation.

Surprisingly, rural tourism turned out to be a priority of Primorsko Municipality. This matter was clarified after the town's mayor Lilqna Dimova represented the program for the fulfillment of Municipality's plan for development until 2013. The construction of yacht harbor and future development of infrastructure at North and South Beach are among the key points. Monitor Daily reported that the ambitious program was completely accepted by Local Parliament. Municipality Primorsko will allot money for the financing of reconstruction of rural houses, creation of eco routes, and also for eco paths to Lavskata Glava, the church "St.Paraskeva" and Maslen Nos.

The goal is to turn villages into a destination for alternative tourism. The construction of bicycle alley from Primorsko to Kiten is being prepared and the re-establishment of Dqvolska River mouth. One of the greatest landmarks of Primorsko sea resort is the natural reserve "Ropotamo" where you can take the opportunity to spend one-hour boat-journey to the mouth of Ropotamo River.

A unique Thracian sanctuary, Begliktash, is located nearby Primorsko, not far away from Duni holiday village. Municipality Primorsko is expected to be the leader of tourism at South Black Sea Region and Strandja Mountain, a stable and self-ruled community, preferred place for development of competitive business, ecological and rural place. In the past, two of the most picturesque and wild beaches at Bulgarian seaside were spread out near Primorsko.

The only one way to spend a couple of nights was either to rent a room in rural house or to choose a hotel in the International Youth Center. Nowadays it is widely known that the situation is rather different. Beaches are not wild anymore and many noisy bars, tempting discos and modern complexes are built. Therefore, Municipality Primorsko has put an emphasis on the development of villages, where tourists can delight in the tranquility and let themselves be enthralled by the simplicity and charm of Bulgarian village

ERTD is a collaborative partnership between 13 training institutions and public/private agencies drawn from 5 countries across Europe. The project is supported by the European Union through the Leonardo da Vinci programme, aimed at improving the vocational education systems of Europe.

The aim of the project is to develop and pilot new learning materials and a new course in rural tourism development which will be delivered on-line to course participants via a virtual campus. The programme will incorporate a variety of learning tasks, including the research, design and promotion of new rural tourism itineraries incorporating case studies to facilitate the learning process. The learning programmes will ensure skills and knowledge of participants meet the needs of the rural tourism sector and new opportunities for employment within it.

The new learning programme developed within this pilot initiative is aimed at the following groups of participants

- Those owner/managers and employees involved in rural tourism activities, eg bed & breakfast, self catering holidays, agro-tourism
- Young people training in Leisure and Tourism
- Those people seeking to set up business within the rural tourism sector including the unemployed and those wishing to change direction

Primary Outcomes of the Project

- New learning programmes, course materials, to meet the needs of rural tourism enterprises which will be piloted, tested and evaluated across participating European countries
- The new courses will be developed using e-learning methodologies and will lead to a 'European' accreditation

and certification offering participants recognition of the skills and competencies acquired. Certification will be secured in the following

- Management in Rural Tourism
- Development of Rural Tourist Attractions

7 FRAMEWORK FOR RURAL TOURISM

Rural tourism typically refers to tourism outside densely-populated areas and tourism centres. In some countries, the term 'farm tourism' (agritourism, agrotourism) is synonymous with rural tourism. Wilderness tourism and forest tourism can, in some contexts, be included in the concept of rural tourism, whereas in some other circumstances these terms can be considered as separate. In many countries, rural tourism is understood to be more or less synonymous with nature tourism or at least travelling in nature, and the 'framework' for rural tourism is usually offered by national parks and other publicly-owned land areas.

We examine the objectives of developing rural tourism from two different perspectives. Firstly, the development of rural tourism is examined in the context of Finnish rural-development policy. Rural policy is commonly seen as holistic, extensive development and it is described as coordinative and integrative. There is no established division between rural policy and rural development. He however, considers the strengthening of the economic activities and peoples' welfare in rural areas as the most-central objectives of this rural policy.

The second perspective is relates to rural entrepreneurs. These two perspectives are considered because the former seeks to create conditions that influence the behaviour of the latter. By appreciating the dynamics of both aspects, there is greater likelihood of developing effective policy interventions.

THE RURAL-DEVELOPMENT PERSPECTIVE

Rural tourism is often seen as one significant means of developing livelihoods particularly in areas with negative population growth. It is believed that rural tourism creates new jobs, decreases migration and helps to maintain the local level of services. According to international research, rural tourism also seems to particularly improve the position of women, as the majority of the tourism businesses in farms are family businesses. Equally, tourism has also increased local demand for primary-production businesses, particularly farm products, in rural areas.

Rural-development strategy objectives generally aim towards the creation and maintenance of new jobs, the expansion of business activities, the support of public services and the creation of new free-time opportunities for travellers. The development of rural tourism often specifically involves the economic and social development of a rural area.

Rural tourism is a relatively small sector of the tourism industry from a global perspective, yet it still has great significance for local economies at many destinations. When the benefits yielded by tourism are generally examined in an area as gross income and person work years, many economic, social and environmental benefits with wider significance receive less attention.

Tourism increases an awareness of, for example, a need for the preservation and development of local culture and can strengthen the local cultural identity. Many services, which also benefit the local population, stay alive with the help of tourism. The success of rural tourism is dependent on an attractive environment, which is why tourism often enhances the protection of nature and culture.

The rural-support programmes targeted inside and also outside the European Union have generated not only large-scale national, but also local rural-tourism development programmes. The development of rural tourism is most successful when it is based on national strategy and co-ordination and strategy with local commitment and local actors. The success of tourism-development plans is dependent on both the administration's ability to support-development projects and the entrepreneurs' desire and ability to commit themselves to the development plans.

Agri-tourism

It is defined most broadly, involves any agriculturally-based operation or activity that brings visitors to a farm or ranch. Agri-tourism has different definitions in different parts of the world, and sometimes refers specifically to farm stays, as in Italy. Elsewhere, agritourism includes a wide variety of activities, including buying produce direct from a farm stand, navigating a corn maze, picking fruit, feeding animals, or staying at a B&B on a farm.

Agri-tourism is a form of niche tourism that is considered a growth industry in many parts of the world, including Australia, Canada, the United States, and the Philippines. Agri-tourism overlaps with geotourism, ecotourism, and culinary tourism. Other terms associated with agritourism are "agritainment", "value added products," "farm direct marketing", and "sustainable agriculture".

Agritourism is widespread in America. Agritourists can choose from a wide range of activities that include picking fruits and vegetables, riding horses, tasting honey, learning about wine and cheesemaking, or shopping in farm gift shops and farm stands for local and regional produce or hand-crafted gifts.

According the USDA, Cooperative State, Education and Extension Service, "Tourism is becoming increasingly important to the U.S. economy. A conservative estimate from the Federal Reserve Board in Kansas, based on 2000 data, shows that basic travel and tourism industries accounted for 3.6 percent of all U.S. employment. Even more telling, data from the Travel Industry Association of America indicate that 1 out of every 18 people in the U.S. has a job directly resulting from travel expenditures."

Through the Small Farm Center at the University of California, "Agricultural tourism or agritourism, is one alternative for improving the incomes and potential economic viability of small farms and rural communities. Some forms of agritourism enterprises are well developed in California, including fairs and festivals. Other possibilities still offer potential for development." The UC Small Farm Center has developed a California Agritourism Database that "provides visitors and potential entrepreneurs with information about existing agritourism locations throughout the state."

In Western North Carolina, the organization HandMade in America is using agritourism to develop their local economy and craft trades, and to educate visitors about agriculture practices. On the web site, *Hand Made in America*, they look at agritourism as a "… niche market not only assists communities with solutions to help diversify their economic base, but it also helps our regional urban centers and increasingly suburban populations to understand the important role that farming and rural life plays in our history, by highlighting the need for it in our contemporary society. Agri-tourism projects reinforce the need to support local growers and sources and allow the visitor to experience what it is to be part of the land…"

The publication *Promoting Tourism in Rural America* explains the need for planning and marketing your rural community and weighing the pros and cons of tourism. According to the publication, local citizen participation is helpful and should be included in starting any kind of a tourism program. Citizen participation in planning tourism can contribute to building a successful program that enhances the community.

Additional websites that promote and publicize agritourism in the United States include Rural Bounty , founded by agritourism consultant Jane Eckert, Sleep in the Hay , a nationwide directory of farm stays, and Farm Stay USA , a blog that profiles farm stays and tracks agritourism news.

PUBLIC AWARENESS

People have become more interested in how their food is produced. They want to meet farmers and processors and talk with them about what goes into food production. For many people who visit farms, especially children, the visit marks the first time they see the source of their food, be it a dairy cow, an ear of corn growing in a field, or an apple they can pick right off a tree.

DUDE RANCHES

Dude (or guest) ranches offer tourists the chance to work on cattle ranches, and sometimes participate in cattle drives. The fact sheet, *Promoting the Farm and Ranch Recreation Business*, gives farmers and ranchers information on marketing and developing strategies to win tourism dollars. Dude ranches are common in the United States and Australian Outback.

Farm Stay

Farm stays have been a growing trend in Europe at least since the 1980s , particularly in Italy, where they are called *agriturismo.* Farm stays are now growing in popularity in other parts of the world as well, especially Australia, Asia, and North America . Reasons for this increasing popularity include farmers' desire for more diverse and dependable income streams and consumers' desire for to reconnect with rural heritage and the food supply.

A farm stay is any type of accommodation on a working farm. Some farm stays may be interactive. Some are family-focused, offering children opportunities to feed animals, collect eggs and learn how a farm functions.. Others don't allow children and instead offer a peaceful retreat for adults. For the accommodations, guests normally pay rates similar to area bed & breakfasts or vacation rentals, although pricing varies considerably.

The term "farm stay" can also describe a work exchange agreement, where the guest works a set number of hours per week in exchange for free or very affordable accommodations, such as those set up through World Wide Opportunities on Organic Farms, or WWOOF.

Possible farm stay accommodations include:

- Cabins
- Cottages
- Converted barns/outbuildings
- Farmhouse guest rooms
- Platform tents
- Tent camping
- Yurts

Farm stays can be described as agritourism (a farmer opening his/her farm to tourists for any reason, including farm stands and u-pick), ecotourism (Responsible travel to natural areas that conserves the environment and improves the well-being of local people), and geotourism (tourism that sustains or enhances the geographical character of a place—its environment, culture, aesthetics, heritage, and the well-being of its residents).

GEO-TOURISM

Geo-tourism is "best practice" tourism that sustains, or even enhances, the geographical character of a place, such as its culture, environment, heritage, and the well-being of its residents. The concept was introduced publicly in a 2002 report by the Travel Industry Association of America (as of 2009 this organization adapted name to U.S. Travel Association) and National Geographic Traveler magazine.

National Geographic senior editor Jonathan B. Tourtellot and his wife, Sally Bensusen, coined the term in 1997 in response to requests for a term and concept more encompassing than *ecotourism* and *sustainable tourism*.

Like ecotourism, geo-tourism promotes a virtuous circle whereby tourism revenues provide a local incentive to protect what tourists are coming to see, but extends the principle beyond nature and ecology to incorporate all characteristics that contribute to *sense of place*, such as historic structures, living and traditional culture, landscapes, cuisine, arts and artisan, as well as local flora and fauna. Geo-tourism incorporates sustainability principles, but in addition to the do-no-harm ethic, geo-tourism focuses on the place as a whole. The idea of enhancement allows for development based on character of place, rather than standardized international branding, and generic architecture, food, and so on.

Geo-tourism Charter

The National Geographic Society defines geotourism as tourism that sustains or enhances the geographical character of a place – its environment, culture, aesthetics, heritage, and the well-being of its residents.

National Geographic Society has also drawn up a "Geotourism Charter" based on 13 principles:

1. **Integrity of place:** Enhance geographical character by developing and improving it in ways distinctive to the local, reflective of its natural and cultural heritage, so as to encourage market differentiation and cultural pride.
2. **International codes:** Adhere to the principles embodied in the World Tourism Organization's Global Code of Ethics for Tourism and the Principles of the Cultural Tourism Charter established by the International Council on Monuments and Sites (ICOMOS).
3. **Market selectivity:** Encourage growth in tourism market segments most likely to appreciate, respect, and disseminate information about the distinctive assets of the locale.
4. **Market diversity:** Encourage a full range of appropriate food and lodging facilities, so as to appeal to the entire demographic spectrum of the geotourism market and so maximize economic resiliency over both the short and long term.

5. **Tourist satisfaction**: Ensure that satisfied, excited geotourists bring new vacation stories home and encourage friends to experience the same thing, thus providing continuing demand for the destination.
6. **Community involvement**: Base tourism on community resources to the extent possible, encouraging local small businesses and civic groups to build partnerships to promote and provide a distinctive, honest visitor experience and market their locales effectively. Help businesses develop approaches to tourism that build on the area's nature, history and culture, including food and drink, artisanry, performance arts, etc.
7. **Community benefit:** Encourage micro- to medium-size enterprises and tourism business strategies that emphasize economic and social benefits to involved communities, especially poverty alleviation, with clear communication of the destination stewardship policies required to maintain those benefits.
8. **Protection and enhancement of destination appeal**: Encourage businesses to sustain natural habitats, heritage sites, aesthetic appeal, and local culture. Prevent degradation by keeping volumes of tourists within maximum acceptable limits. Seek business models that can operate profitably within those limits. Use persuasion, incentives, and legal enforcement as needed.
9. **Land use**: Anticipate development pressures and apply techniques to prevent undesired overdevelopment and degradation. Contain resort and vacation-home sprawl, especially on coasts and islands, so as to retain a diversity of natural and scenic environments and ensure continued resident access to waterfronts. Encourage major self-contained tourism attractions, such as large-scale theme parks and convention centers unrelated to character of place, to be sited in needier locations with no significant ecological, scenic, or cultural assets.

10. **Conservation of resources**: Encourage businesses to minimize water pollution, solid waste, energy consumption, water usage, landscaping chemicals, and overly bright nighttime lighting. Advertise these measures in a way that attracts the large, environmentally sympathetic tourist market.
11. **Planning**: Recognize and respect immediate economic needs without sacrificing long-term character and the geotourism potential of the destination. Where tourism attracts in-migration of workers, develop new communities that themselves constitute a destination enhancement. Strive to diversify the economy and limit population influx to sustainable levels. Adopt public strategies for mitigating practices that are incompatible with geotourism and damaging to the image of the destination.
12. **Interactive interpretation**: Engage both visitors and hosts in learning about the place. Encourage residents to promote the natural and cultural heritage of their communities so tourists gain a richer experience and residents develop pride in their locales.
13. **Evaluation**: Establish an evaluation process to be conducted on a regular basis by an independent panel representing all stakeholder interests, and publicize evaluation results.

Wilderness Hut

A wilderness hut is a rent-free, open dwelling place for temporary accommodation, usually located in wilderness areas, national parks and along backpacking routes. As such, the tradition is largely found in Finland, and to some extent in Sweden, Norway, and northern Russia too.

The huts can be divided into official and unofficial, or maintained and unmaintained ones. Official wilderness huts are mostly maintained by Metsähallitus (Finnish for *Administration of Forests*), the Finnish state-owned forest management company.

Most of the wilderness huts in Finland are situated in the northern and eastern parts of the country. Their size can vary greatly: the Lahtinen cottage in the Muotkatunturi Wilderness Area can barely hold two people, whereas the Luirojärvi cottage in the Urho Kekkonen National Park can hold as many as 16.

A wilderness hut need not be reserved beforehand, and they are open for everyone.

For centuries the vast wildernesses of Finland and its resources were divided amongst the Finnish agricultural societies (such as families, villages, parishes, and provinces) for the purpose of collecting resources. Areas owned in this way were called *erämaa*, literally "portion-land". People from agricultural societies made trips to their *erämaas* in summer, mainly to trap fur-bearing animals but also to hunt game, fish, and collect taxes from the local hunter-fisher population.

Huts were built in the wilderness for use as base camps for hunters and fishers from agricultural societies. Also non-agricultural Sami people built huts to help them manage reindeer. The earliest huts, were meant only for the use of people from the society that owned them. People from other societies were not allowed to use the resources of other societies' *erämaas*.

Huts that were free for everyone were first seen in late 18th century Finland, when dwelling places were built along walking routes for passers-by. In the 19th century the authorities started building these huts. Later in the 20th century they started to be built for travellers.

CUSTOMS

A Finnish wilderness hut typically contains at least a dining table, a gas stove and a heating stove. The wilderness hut commission of Lapland Province wrote these "unwritten laws of the wilderness" in the mid-20th century:

- Anyone who steals or deliberately destroys or damages other people's property behind an unlocked door not only commits a crime but also a shameful and cowardly act. So leave the contents of the cottage in good shape when you leave. This means that, should you return to the cottage, they will be in good condition. Huts can (and will) be locked if there's ill conduct.

- When you enter the cottage, check that the fireplace is in safe and in good working order before you light a fire. If there is a problem and you cannot fix it, leave a message detailing the problem, so that the owner will know about it and can fix it.
- Use the firewood reserves of the cottage sparingly unless you can immediately obtain new billets, as the next visitor may have an urgent need of dry wood. It is obvious that whittling kindling out of bunk boards, to say nothing of burning them, is an outrageous infringement of the laws of the wilderness.
- Use the cottage's food and other emergency supplies only in a really urgent situation. Another passer-by may later perish without them.
- Keep the cottage tidy, and the surroundings and the water supply clean. Leave the trees around the cottage in peace.
- Upon leaving the cottage, clean it well and provide it with at least the same amount of firewood that you have burned. A good traveller leaves a plentiful supply of billets and, if the stocks are low, replenishes them.
- If there is a guestbook in the cottage, leave your name, the date and words about your trip. Do not carve your initials in the walls of the cottage; this is an ugly habit that should be broken.
- If you can, leave a box of matches, dry kindling, bread, salt, or other non-perishable food in the cottage, perhaps in a bag hanging from the ceiling, safe from mice.
- Before you close the door make sure that the fire in the fireplace has completely died out and that there is no danger of it restarting.

- The last person to arrive at the cottage has a greater right to use it than those already dwelling there. So, if the cottage cannot hold everyone, those who have stayed there the longest are obliged to make room for those just arriving and tired. The old Finnish saying must be remembered: *Sopu sijaa antaa* (Harmony gives room). Also, note the American saying: "First in, first out".
- Lastly: never rely solely on the wilderness huts while hiking, on the popular routes they may be crowded. Always carry a tent or some cloth applicable to making a shelter.

8 Effective Marketing for Rural Tourism

When making the choice to take a vacation for rural tourism, it is nice to have information available about the location. People often look to chambers of commerce or a city Web site for this information. These are highly useful tools for what is known as tourism marketing.

What is Tourism Marketing?

As cities and regions want to attract more visitors, they look for creative and effective ways to let travelers know what attractions and amenities they offer. This is tourism marketing.

What Should Tourism Marketing Include?

For tourism marketing to be successful and effective, it needs to serve the needs of the visitor it is trying to attract and the organization producing the material.

What is the Point of Tourism Marketing?

The point of these marketing resources is to promote what the resort, city, state or region has to offer in an appealing, yet honest manner.

Things to Consider When Creating a Campaign

It is important to highlight the desirable aspects of a location without making too lofty promises or painting an unrealistic picture for the tourist. This will lead to less tourism in the long run.

How Does One Measure its Success?

Ultimately, a successful tourism marketing campaign is able to provide economic benefits for those who live in the area while attracting visitors, new citizens and businesses.

TOURISM MARKETING ON INTERNET

eTourism Marketing Consultants specialise in Internet Marketing for Tourism Organsiations ranging from small hotels to multinational travel companies. Some of the solutions that we offer are: Online Advertising Search Engine Marketing (SEM)Search Engine Optimisation (SEO)Affiliate MarketingEmail MarketingCustomer Relationship Management (CRM)Website Development and Designing.Online DistributionSoftware and Application development.

Email Marketing

Email marketing is a form of direct marketing which uses electronic mail as a means of communicating commercial or fund-raising messages to an audience. In its broadest sense, every email sent to a potential or current customer could be considered email marketing. However, the term is usually used to refer to:

- sending email messages with the purpose of enhancing the relationship of a merchant with its current or previous customers, to encourage customer loyalty and repeat business,
- sending email messages with the purpose of acquiring new customers or convincing current customers to purchase something immediately,
- adding advertisements to email messages sent by other companies to their customers, and

- sending email messages over the Internet, as email did and does exist outside the Internet (e.g., network email and FIDO).

Researchers estimate that United States firms alone spent US $400 million on email marketing in 2006.

COMPARISON TO TRADITIONAL MAIL

There are both advantages and disadvantages to using email marketing in comparison to traditional advertising mail.

Advantages

Email marketing (on the Internet) is popular with companies for several reasons:

- An exact return on investment can be tracked ("track to basket") and has proven to be high when done properly. Email marketing is often reported as second only to search marketing as the most effective online marketing tactic.
- Advertisers can reach substantial numbers of email subscribers who have opted in (i.e., consented) to receive email communications on subjects of interest to them.
- Over half of Internet users check or send email on a typical day.
- Email is popular with digital marketers, rising an estimated 15% in 2009 to £292m in the UK.

Disadvantages

A report issued by the email services company Return Path, as of mid-2008 email deliverability is still an issue for legitimate marketers. According to the report, legitimate email servers averaged a delivery rate of 56%; twenty percent of the messages were rejected, and eight percent were filtered.

Companies considering the use of an email marketing program must make sure that their program does not violate spam laws such as the United States' Controlling the Assault of Non-Solicited

Pornography and Marketing Act (CAN-SPAM), the European Privacy and Electronic Communications Regulations 2003, or their Internet service provider's acceptable use policy.

OPT-IN EMAIL ADVERTISING

Opt-in email advertising, or permission marketing, is a method of advertising via email whereby the recipient of the advertisement has consented to receive it. This method is one of several developed by marketers to eliminate the disadvantages of email marketing.

Opt-in email marketing may evolve into a technology that uses a handshake protocol between the sender and receiver. This system is intended to eventually result in a high degree of satisfaction between consumers and marketers. If opt-in email advertising is used, the material that is emailed to consumers will be "anticipated". It is assumed that the consumer wants to receive it, which makes it unlike unsolicited advertisements sent to the consumer. Ideally, opt-in email advertisements will be more personal and relevant to the consumer than untargeted advertisements.

A common example of permission marketing is a newsletter sent to an advertising firm's customers. Such newsletters inform customers of upcoming events or promotions, or new products. In this type of advertising, a company that wants to send a newsletter to their customers may ask them at the point of purchase if they would like to receive the newsletter.

With a foundation of opted-in contact information stored in their database, marketers can send out promotional materials automatically—known as Drip Marketing. They can also segment their promotions to specific market segments.

LEGAL REQUIREMENTS

In 2002 the European Union introduced the Directive on Privacy and Electronic Communications. Article 13 of the Directive prohibits the use of email addresses for marketing purposes. The

Directive establishes the opt-in regime, where unsolicited emails may be sent only with prior agreement of the recipient.

The directive has since been incorporated into the laws of member states. In the UK it is covered under the Privacy and Electronic Communications (EC Directive) Regulations 2003 and applies to all organisations that send out marketing by some form of electronic communication.

The CAN-SPAM Act of 2003 authorizes a US $16,000 penalty per violation for spamming each individual recipient. Therefore, many commercial email marketers within the United States utilize a service or special software to ensure compliance with the Act. A variety of older systems exist that do not ensure compliance with the Act. To comply with the Act's regulation of commercial email, services typically require users to authenticate their return address and include a valid physical address, provide a one-click unsubscribe feature, and prohibit importing lists of purchased addresses that may not have given valid permission.

In addition to satisfying legal requirements, email service providers (ESPs) began to help customers establish and manage their own email marketing campaigns. The service providers supply email templates and general best practices, as well as methods for handling subscriptions and cancellations automatically. Some ESPs will provide insight/assistance with deliverability issues for major email providers. They also provide statistics pertaining to the number of messages received and opened, and whether the recipients clicked on any links within the messages.

The CAN-SPAM Act was updated with some new regulations including a no fee provision for opting out, further definition of "sender", post office or private mail boxes count as a "valid physical postal address" and definition of "person". These new provisions went into effect on July 7, 2008.

CAN-SPAM does not pre-empt state laws that prohibit falsity and deception in email messages. Some states allow recipients of false and deceptive email messages to sue the the business whose products are advertised in the false or deceptive email. Examples of falsity and deception in emails include false header information, advertising products as free when they are not, misrepresenting the source of the email, unauthorized use of third party domain names, and misleading or blank subject lines.

Advertising Mail

Advertising mail, also known as direct mail, junk mail, or admail, is the delivery of advertising material to recipients of postal mail. The delivery of advertising mail forms a large and growing service for many postal services, and direct-mail marketing forms a significant portion of the direct marketing industry. Some organizations attempt to help people opt out of receiving advertising mail, in many cases motivated by a concern over its negative environmental impact.

Advertising mail includes advertising circulars, catalogs, CDs, "pre-approved" credit card applications, and other commercial merchandising materials delivered to both homes and businesses. It may be addressed to pre-selected individuals, or unaddressed and delivered on a neighbourhood-by-neighbourhood basis.

Postal systems have enacted lower rates for buyers of bulk mail permits. In order to qualify for these rates, marketers must format and sort the mail in specific ways – which reduces the handling required by the postal service.

Income from advertising mail represents a significant and growing portion of some postal services' budgets, and it is a service actively marketed by them. In Canada, addressed and unaddressed advertising mail accounted for 20% of Canada Post's revenue in 2005, and the share is increasing. Postal services employ the terms *advertising mail*, *admail*, and *direct mail*, while avoiding and objecting to the pejorative term *junk mail*.

In many developed countries, advertising mail represents a significant and growing amount of the total volume of mail. In the United States, "Standard mail: advertising" comprised 29% of all mail in 1980 and 43% in 2003.

DIRECT MAIL MARKETING

Direct mail is a common form of direct marketing, and may be employed by for-profit businesses, charities and other non-profits, political campaigns, and other organizations. Advertisers often refine direct mail practices into *targeted mailing*, in which mail is sent out following database analysis to select recipients considered most likely to respond positively. For example a person who has demonstrated an interest in golf may receive direct mail for golf related products or perhaps for goods and services that are appropriate for golfers. This use of database analysis is a type of database marketing.

Alternatively, unaddressed direct mail may be sent on a neighbourhood-by-neighbourhood basis. Whether at the individual or neighbourhood level, direct mail marketing allows recipients to be targeted, attempting to match the demographic profile of the recipients to one most closely matching that of likely customers. Individually targeted direct mail may be tailored based on previous transactions and gathered data. For example, all male recipients of an offer may receive a personalized package with a man's picture on the cover, while all female recipients receive a picture of a woman.

Political Usage

Political campaigns make frequent use of direct mail, both to gain votes from the electorate as a whole, and to target certain groups of voters thought to be open to a candidate's message and to appeal for campaign funds.

Certain organizations and individuals have become known for their prowess in direct mail, including in the U.S., the Free Congress Foundation in the 1970s, Response Dynamics, Inc. in the 1980s, the National Congressional Club, and Richard Viguerie. With the advent of the Internet in political campaigns, direct mail became just one of many campaign management tools, but still played a significant role.

Business-to-Business mailings (B2B)

When targeted to other businesses rather than individuals, direct mail is known as a *business to business* mailing. Traditionally, this worked in one of two ways: as a direct sale, therefore precluding the use of a salesperson or a retail store, or as a method of generating leads for a salesforce. The former method was ideally used by products that were easy to sell, were familiar to the prospect and needed no demonstration. The latter method was used for large-ticket items or for those that needed demonstration for example.

One method of direct mailing used in B2B is known as "bill-me". In this direct-mail marketing offer, the buyer is shipped the product prior to payment and then is sent an invoice later.

OPTING OUT

Several organizations offer opt-out services to people who wish to reduce or eliminate the amount of addressed advertising mail they receive. In the United Kingdom, the Mailing Preference Service allows people to register with them for removal from posted as opposed to hand-delivered mail. In the United States, there are several nonprofit organizations, such as 41pounds.org, catalogchoice.org, as well as private sector alternatives like Greendimes.

In response to a US Supreme Court ruling (Rowan v. Post Office Dept.), the United States Postal Service enables an applicant to obtain a *Prohibitory Order*, which gives people the power to stop non-governmental organizations from sending them mail, and to demand such organizations remove the consumers' information from their mailing lists.

In Canada, the highly-publicized Red Dot Campaign offers advice on reducing unaddressed advertising mail. The campaign focuses on advertising the Canada Post policy to respect "No Junkmail" signs, noting that this policy is not promoted by Canada Post itself. The name "red dot" refers to an internal marker used by Canada Post to indicate which households do not wish to receive unaddressed admail.

The UK Royal Mail also offers an opt-out service, though it sparked public outrage by warning that unaddressed government mailings could not be separated from advertisements, and those who opted out of the latter would stop receiving the former as well. Several websites critical of junk mail have guides for people interested in reducing the amount of junk mail they get, such as the Center for a New American Dream

ENVIRONMENTAL EFFECT

Several of the above organizations, as well as environmental groups, express concern about the environmental impact generated by junk mail. In the United States, the Environmental Protection Agency estimates that 44% of junk mail is discarded without being opened or read, equaling four million tons of waste paper per year, with 32% recovered for recycling. Further, the Ohio Office of Compliance Assistance and Pollution Prevention (OCAPP) estimates that 250,000 homes could be heated for a single day's junk mail.

In the United Kingdom, the Minister of State responsible for the Department for Environment, Food and Rural Affairs estimated that "direct mail and promotions" accounted for between 500,000 and 600,000 tonnes of paper in 2002, with 13% being recycled. The government and the Direct Marketing Association (UK) together agreed on recycling targets for the direct mail industry, including a goal of 55% by 2009, though the DMA's latest estimates are that the industry will fall well short of this mark.

Direct Marketing

Direct marketing is a form of advertising that reaches its audience without using traditional formal channels of advertising, such as TV, newspapers or radio. Businesses communicate straight to the consumer with advertising techniques such as fliers, catalogue distribution, promotional letters, and street advertising.

Direct Advertising is a sub-discipline and type of marketing. There are two main definitional characteristics which distinguish it from other types of marketing. The first is that it sends its message directly to consumers, without the use of intervening commercial communication media.

The second characteristic is the core principle of successful Advertising driving a specific "call to action." This aspect of direct marketing involves an emphasis on trackable, measurable, positive responses from consumers (known simply as "response" in the industry) regardless of medium. If the advertisement asks the prospect to take a specific action, for instance call a free phone number or visit a Web site, then the effort is considered to be direct response advertising.

Direct marketing is predominantly used by small to medium-size enterprises with limited advertising budgets that do not have a well-recognized brand message. A well-executed direct advertising campaign can offer a positive return on investment as the message is not hidden with overcomplicated branding. Instead, direct advertising is straight to the point; offers a product, service, or event; and explains how to get the offered product, service, or event.

The term *direct marketing* is believed to have been first used in 1967 in a speech by Lester Wunderman, who pioneered direct marketing techniques with brands such as American Express and Columbia Records. The term *junk mail*, referring to unsolicited commercial ads delivered via post office or directly deposited in consumers' mail boxes, can be traced back to 1954. The term spam, meaning "unsolicited commercial e-mail," can be traced back to March 31, 1993, although in its first few months it merely referred to inadvertently posting a message so many times on UseNet that the repetitions effectively drowned out the normal flow of conversation.

Although Wunderman may have been the first to use the term *direct marketing*, the practice of mail order selling (direct marketing via mail) essentially began in the U.S. upon invention of the typewriter in 1867. The first modern mail-order catalog was produced by Aaron Montgomery Ward in 1872. The Direct Mail

Advertising Association, predecessor of the present-day Direct Marketing Association, was first established in 1917. Third class bulk mail postage rates were established in 1928.

Direct marketing's history in Europe can be traced to the 15th century. Upon Gutenberg's invention of movable type, the first trade catalogs from printer-publishers appeared sometime around 1450.

BENEFITS AND DRAWBACKS

Direct marketing is attractive to many marketers, because in many cases its positive effect (but not negative results) can be measured directly. For example, if a marketer sends out 1,000 solicitations by mail, and 100 respond to the promotion, the marketer can say with confidence that campaign led directly to 10% direct responses. The number of recipients who are offended by junk mail/spam, however, is not easily measured. By contrast, measurement of other media must often be indirect, since there is no direct response from a consumer. Measurement of results, a fundamental element in successful direct marketing, is explored in greater detail elsewhere in this article.

The Internet has made it easier for marketing managers to measure the results of a campaign. This is often achieved by using a specific Web site landing page directly relating to the promotional material, a call to action will ask the consumer to visit the landing page, and the effectiveness of the campaign can be measured by taking the number of promotional messages distributed (e.g., 1,000) and dividing it by the number of responses (people visiting the unique Web site page).

Another way to measure the results is to compare the projected sales for a given term with the actual sales after a direct advertising campaign. While many marketers recognize the financial benefits of increasing targeted awareness, some direct marketing efforts using particular media have been criticized for generating unwanted solicitations, not due to the method of communication but because of poorly compiled demographic databases, advertisers do not wish to waste money on communicating with consumers not interested in their products.

For example, direct mail that is irrelevant to the recipient is considered "junk mail," and unwanted e-mail messages are considered "spam." Some consumers are demanding an end to direct marketing for privacy and environmental reasons which direct marketers are able to do to some extent by using "opt-out" lists, variable printing, and more-targeted mailing lists.

In response to consumer demand and increasing business pressure to increase the effectiveness of reaching the right consumer with direct marketing, companies specialize in targeted direct advertising to great effect, reducing advertising budget waste and increasing the effectiveness of delivering a marketing message with better geodemography information, delivering the advertising message to only the consumers interested in the product, service, or event on offer.

CHANNELS

Direct Mail

The most common form of direct marketing is direct mail sometimes called junk mail, used by advertisers who send paper mail to all postal customers in an area or to all customers on a list.

Any low-budget medium that can be used to deliver a communication to a customer can be employed in direct marketing. Probably the most commonly used medium for direct marketing is mail, in which marketing communications are sent to customers using the postal service. The term direct mail is used in the direct marketing industry to refer to communication deliveries by the Post Office, which may also be referred to as "junk mail" or "admail" and may involve bulk mail.

Direct mail includes advertising circulars, catalogs, free trial CDs, pre-approved credit card applications, and other unsolicited merchandising invitations delivered by mail or to homes and businesses, or delivered to consumers' mailboxes by delivery services other than the Post Office. Bulk mailings are a particularly popular method of promotion for businesses operating in the financial services, home computer, and travel and tourism industries.

In many developed countries, direct mail represents such a significant amount of the total volume of mail that special rate classes have been established. In the United States and United Kingdom, for example, there are bulk mail rates that enable marketers to send mail at rates that are substantially lower than regular first-class rates. In order to qualify for these rates, marketers must format and sort the mail in particular ways – which reduces the handling (and therefore costs) required by the postal service.

Advertisers often refine direct mail practices into *targeted mailing*, in which mail is sent out following database analysis to select recipients considered most likely to respond positively. For example a person who has demonstrated an interest in golf may receive direct mail for golf related products or perhaps for goods and services that are appropriate for golfers. This use of database analysis is a type of database marketing. The United States Postal Service calls this form of mail "advertising mail".

Telemarketing

Another common form of direct marketing is telemarketing, in which marketers contact consumers by phone. The unpopularity of cold call telemarketing (in which the consumer does not expect or invite the sales call) has led some US states and the US federal government to create "no-call lists" and legislation including heavy fines. This process may be outsourced to specialist call centres.

In the US, a national do-not-call list went into effect on October 1, 2003. Under the law, it is illegal for telemarketers to call anyone who has registered themselves on the list. After the list had operated for one year, over 62 million people had signed up. The telemarketing industry opposed the creation of the list, but most telemarketers have complied with the law and refrained from calling people who are on the list. Canada has passed legislation to create a similar Do Not Call List. In other countries it is voluntary, such as the New Zealand Name Removal Service.

Email Marketing

Email Marketing is a third type of direct marketing. A major concern is spam. As a result of the proliferation of mass spamming, ISPs and email service providers have developed increasingly effective E-Mail Filtering programs. These filters can interfere with the delivery of email marketing campaigns, even if the person has subscribed to receive them, as legitimate email marketing can possess the same hallmarks as spam. There are a range of e-mail service providers that provide services for legitimate opt-in emailers to avoid being classified as spam.

Door-to-Door Leaflet Marketing

Leaflet distribution services are used extensively by the fast food industries, and many other business focussing on a local catchment. Business to consumer business model, similar to direct mail marketing, this method is targeted purely by area, and costs a fraction of the amount of a mailshot due to not having to purchase stamps, envelopes or having to buy address lists and the names of home occupants.

Broadcast Faxing

A fourth type of direct marketing, broadcast faxing, is now less common than the other forms. This is partly due to laws in the United States and elsewhere which make it illegal.

Voicemail Marketing

A fifth type of direct marketing has emerged out of the market prevalence of personal voice mailboxes, and business voicemail systems. Due to the ubiquity of email marketing, and the expense of direct mail and telemarketing, voicemail marketing presented a cost effective means by which to reach people directly, by voice.

Abuse of consumer marketing applications of voicemail marketing resulted in an abundance of "voice-spam", and prompted many jurisdictions to pass laws regulating consumer voicemail marketing.

More recently, businesses have utilized guided voicemail (an application where pre-recorded voicemails are guided by live callers) to accomplish personalized business-to-business marketing formerly reserved for telemarketing. Because guided voicemail is used to contact only businesses, it is exempt from Do Not Call regulations in place for other forms of voicemail marketing.

Another variation is voicemail courier (an application where pre-recorded voice messages are couriered into voicemail by live callers) to accomplish personalized voicemail marketing. Voicemail courier is used for both business-to-business marketing and also business-to-consumer applications.

Couponing

Couponing is used in print media to elicit a response from the reader. An example is a coupon which the reader cuts out and presents to a super-store check-out counter to avail of a discount. Coupons in newspapers and magazines cannot be considered direct marketing, since the marketer incurs the cost of supporting a third-party medium (the newspaper or magazine); direct marketing aims to circumvent that balance, paring the costs down to solely delivering their unsolicited sales message to the consumer, without supporting the newspaper that the consumer seeks and welcomes.

Direct-response Television Marketing

Direct marketing on TV (commonly referred to as DRTV) has two basic forms: long form (usually half-hour or hour-long segments that explain a product in detail and are commonly referred to as infomercials) and short form, which refers to typical 30-second or 60-second commercials that ask viewers for an immediate response (typically to call a phone number on screen or go to a Web site).

TV-response marketing—i.e. infomercials—can be considered a form of direct marketing, since responses are in the form of calls to telephone numbers given on-air. This both allows marketers to reasonably conclude that the calls are due to a particular campaign, and allows the marketers to obtain customers' phone numbers as targets for telemarketing.

Under the Federal Do-Not-Call List rules in the US, if the caller buys anything, the marketer would be exempt from Do-Not-Call List restrictions for a period of time due to having a prior business relationship with the caller. Firms such as QVC, Thane Direct, and Interwood Marketing Group then cross-sell and up-sell to these respondents.

One of the most famous DRTV commercials was for Ginsu Knives by Ginsu Products, Inc. of RI. Several aspects of ad, such as its use of adding items to the offer and the guarantee of satisfaction were much copied and came to be considered part of the formula for success with short-form direct-response TV ads (DRTV)

Direct Selling

Direct selling is the sale of products by face-to-face contact with the customer, either by having salespeople approach potential customers in person, or through indirect means such as Tupperware parties.

Popularity of Direct Advertising

A report produced by the Direct Marketing Association found that 57% of the campaigns studied were employing integrated strategies. Of those, almost half (47%) launched with a direct mail campaign, typically followed by e-mail and then telemarketing.

The CO_2 emissions from 41 pounds of advertising mail received annually by the average United States consumer is about 47.6 kilograms (105 pounds) according to one study. The loss of natural habitat potential from the 41 pounds of advertising mail is estimated to be 36.6 square meters (396 square feet).

In the United States many commercial envelope printing companies are moving towards water-based or vegetable-based ink and laminates, and have increased the use of recycled paper.

9 Co-operative Marketing Structure in Rural Tourism

People have formed co-operative groupings in both an informal and formal capacity since man has inhabited the earth. Co-operation is also common between many other living organisms and in some cases culminating in symbiosis and partnership such as that between the egret and water buffalo in the animal kingdom and between lichens and algae in the plant kingdom. However, in all cases the benefit of co-operation must provide a value which is recognised by each co-operative member.

Co-operation can be defined as "groups of independent businesses which recognise the advantage of developing markets jointly rather than in isolation but may be unable to directly appropriate the benefits of co-operative activities... they are tied in a loose way". Morrison (1998) identified the importance of co-operation in the tourism sector particularly for those who are located in a peripheral region or area. She defines co-operation as that which is 'between one or more tourist product providers, whereby each partner seeks to add to its marketing competencies by combining some, but not all of their resources with those of its partners for mutual benefit'. Gray (1985) identified five critical characteristics of collaboration necessary to ensure that working together is successful. These include:

- interdependency of the stakeholder whereby an incentive is required to induce participation;
- joint ownership of decisions;
- solutions emerging by dealing constructively with differences;
- collective responsibility for future direction; and
- the recognition that collaboration is a dynamic, emergent process.

Co-operation can lead to networking opportunities such as economies of scale, access to professional marketing expertise, the development of technology and distribution networks, educational and training support and pooled financial resources. Development of cohesiveness over time within a co-operative can be helped by several factors. Palmer *et al.* (2000) found that similarity of work, group size, threats from outside, leadership style and common social factors such as age, race and social structure could contribute to cohesiveness.

Two of the case studies focus on same product provision though the structural approach of the co-operative is different. Case one considers the individual product provider an individual member and in Case two a designated area made up of a number of product providers constitutes a member. Case three focuses on individual provider membership though reflects the diversity of rural tourism provision within a county delineated geographical area. Factors and inhibitors for successful co-operation are explored.

TOURISM IN IRELAND

The tourism sector in Ireland (a country with a population four million) has had a substantial impact on the national economy over the past fifteen years. The sector has seen unprecedented growth in both visitor numbers and revenue, with over six million overseas visitors generating revenue of 3.2bn in 2002 (or almost 4bn taking into account carrier receipts). In 2002 it supported

140,000 jobs and contributed 4.4 per cent to GNP, making it the most successful-ever 'indigenous' industry .

However, the publication of *New Horizons for Irish Tourism – An Agenda for Action* (DAST, 2003) published in September 2003 acknowledged that the industry was at a crossroads. Although there was still significant satisfaction with the Irish rural tourism product expressed by visitors, there had been a decline, particularly in relation to their perception of value for money, with Ireland considered by some to be an expensive destination. The *Agenda* document set out a strategy to regain competitiveness and to continue to emphasise the importance of 'People, Place and Pace' – elements that have been identified as the main attractors for the country. On the supply side, both underutilised capacity and falling margins have been problems, and a number of key drivers, including marketing and promotion, were identified to combat these.

Structural changes in the administration, management and marketing of tourism have been put in place. The Northern Ireland Peace Process has acted as a catalyst for change whereby Ireland is now marketed as an all-Ireland destination incorporating Northern Ireland, which is under the governance of the UK.

Tourism in Ireland grew through the 1960s and 1970s, but it was in the mid 1980s, after the publication of the first White Paper for tourism in 1985, that the industry took a more strategic approach to both its development and marketing. The rural tourism industry in Ireland is dominated by small and medium enterprises as well as by sole traders, with many of them operating as part-time tourism providers.

Entering into co-operative networks can enable small- and medium-size firms to pool their resources in order to increase their competitiveness, draw up strategic management and marketing plans, reduce operating costs and increase know-how (Buhalis & Cooper, 1998, cited in Hall, 2000). With over 80 percent of tourism enterprises in Ireland constituting of small and medium enterprises, and many of these enterprises in isolated areas, the focus moved from individual marketing to the development of same product and destination marketing co-operatives.

Rural Tourism in Ireland

Rural tourism is defined in Ireland specifically as 'rural areas/ towns with less than 1500 people'. The EU definition of rural tourism is "a holiday that is primarily motivated by the desire to closely experience the countryside, its people, heritage and way of life. The holiday should be primarily based in a rural setting, as opposed to being general touring/sightseeing holiday." (Failte Ireland pers comm.)2004). It is this definition that is used by the National Tourist Board. 'Agritourism', however, is quite specific and in terms of the Irish situation it tends to be linked directly to on-farm activities or accommodation. Grant aid in relation to agritourism was allocated to farmers or in the case of a group application, farmers were required to be part of the applicant group.

Due to the fragmented nature of the rural tourism product, it is difficult to ascertain its worth to the economy. Estimates have suggested 30 per cent of the total value of tourism, or about 1bn in 2002. *Teagasc* are the Farm Advisory Body and are involved in providing advice and training to the rural and farming community. They cite four important factors which need to be addressed in order that growth is sustained: quality, uniqueness, the adoption of an innovative approach, and the importance of training.

Teagasc provides information on its website for the setting up of alternative enterprises including rural tourism, self-catering, B&B, angling, walking and visitor attractions. In the 1960s, due to the decreasing viability of agriculture and the increasing number of tourists to Ireland, farmers were urged to look at developing alternative enterprises to support farm incomes. Tourism bodies encouraged the opening of farm house accommodation. From the early 1970s until the mid-1980s, price supports in agriculture and industry did well. The state did not need to involve itself with land structure or reform within agriculture as it was a reasonably viable sector. Private investment took place and there was no real integration between agriculture and other sectors, as it held its own.

From mid-1980s to the early 1990s, reform of the Common Agricultural Policy and the introduction of milk quotas caused a fall in incomes for some farmers. Rural tourism development now looked more attractive. The mid-1980s saw a drive to develop and invest in tourism in Ireland and to increase visitor numbers. Grant aid from different sources, though primarily from the EU, such as the Operational Programme for Tourism, Operational Programme for Agri-tourism grant and LEADER programme grant aid, encouraged development and marketing in a diverse range of rural tourism products such as equestrian facilities, open visitor farms, golf facilities and accommodation.

The revitalisation of rural areas well complements present tourism objectives, which includes a more equitable regional distribution of visitors throughout the country. Scenic rural areas in Ireland also tend to be areas of agricultural disadvantage, and hence the farming community now often looks towards rural tourism as a source of supplementing income. Rural tourism has helped to sustain agriculture and boost local related industries. It has also been a catalyst in the creation of jobs through direct and related enterprises.

Development of Rural Tourism

There are a number of bodies involved in the development and marketing of rural tourism in Ireland. *Teagasc* is the farm advisory board and employs a rural tourism specialist based in County Galway. County council and county tourism committees are involved in the development and marketing of rural tourism at county level and they contribute to the work undertaken by the regional tourism authorities.

The six regional tourism authorities develop, service and promote tourism in a regional context. Shannon Development operates in this capacity in the mid-West of the country. There are at present 38 LEADER+ companies in the Republic of Ireland which are involved in development, marketing and training in all sectors of rural development. Under LEADER 2, 22.6% of funds were allocated to rural tourism which was significantly more than any other measure (Kearney 2000). LEADER+ presently allocates funding to projects where there is a proven market demand. In a national capacity, *Failte Ireland*, (the National Tourism Board and Tourism Training Authority) employs a product development officer whose remit it is to help develop, market and give advice to the rural tourism sector.

Marketing of Rural Tourism

The marketing of rural tourism is undertaken by a number of bodies. County tourism committees and regional tourism authorities focus on destination marketing within a county and regional context. Irish Farmhouse Holidays (IFH) and Irish Country Holidays (ICH) co-operatively market the farm accommodation sector: both offer bed and breakfast, and ICH additionally offers self-catering accommodation. Product marketing groupings (PMGs) have emerged at county, regional and national levels, and many of these contribute to the rural tourism experience. Operating criteria for these groupings are mainly linked to quality standards. The accommodation sector has strict criteria which lead to approval by the national tourist board.

In this sector, marketing co-operatives have been in existence for many years and criteria focus on the tangible aspects of accommodation delivery. Within the other activities and attractions sectors, criteria are not as clear. If there is a regulatory body, such as AIRE (Association of Irish Riding Establishments) in the case of the equestrian product, those that participate in the product marketing group have to adhere to the agreed regulations. In the case of other activities, such as gardens/heritage houses, there are no regulatory bodies, criteria are vague and products are diverse. Time in operation, standard of product, capability of attracting visitors and availability of facilities for visitor use are mentioned, although those members that are part of the groups may sometimes not fulfil all the criteria.

At a national level, *Failte Ireland* advocates that co-operative marketing opportunities are the most effective means of accessing overseas markets in a cost-effective manner. With this in mind, product marketing groups have been developed in many different products.

In 1999, the Small- and Medium-Sized Accommodation Marketing Initiative was launched to improve the marketing and competitive capabilities of the smaller accommodation enterprises. Administered by the National Tourist Board, this initially focused on the bed and breakfast sector but has since been extended to all sectors of SME accommodation. Its main objectives include the following:

- provision of support for the smaller accommodation sector;
- creation of greater cohesion within the sector;
- creation of awareness and knowledge of individual and co-operative marketing efforts; and
- encouragement of more marketing activity by both associations and groups with industry and the regional tourism authorities.

Tourism Ireland Limited focuses on international marketing and is involved with marketing Ireland abroad as an all Ireland destination. Product quality and cost competitiveness are emphasised as an essential element of the attractiveness of Ireland as a tourism destination.

Barriers and Problems in Relation to Rural Tourism in Ireland

One of the main problems of rural tourism in Ireland is the fragmented nature of the product. Many of those involved in providing a rural tourism experience to the visitor are part-time, either in terms of working hours or in terms of the focus of the enterprise. A wide range of different organisations deliver different elements of the product, and at times organisations that are involved within the sector are accused of lacking co-ordination.

The need for a common ground to facilitate consensus and implement collaborative results requires a more integrated approach based on regular communication and shared values. Due to seasonality factors such as climate, lack of daylight hours, traditional holiday taking patterns, irregular profit margins result. This is exacerbated by the fact that employment may only be seasonal and part-time and thus seen as supplemental rather than central to the business or income stream.

The fragmented nature of the business also contributes to the overall lack of vision, direction and image of the sector as perceived by those working in the industry. Changes in perception have been noted over the past fourteen years during periods of close contact while working with product providers in the rural tourism sector. Gradually with the advent of greater co-operation, it is hoped that this will change. Rural tourism has gone through a cycle over the past ten years.

During the 1990s a vision had been identified for the product, yet those delivering focused mainly on the accommodation provision element of the experience. Open farms, walking, cycling and other such rural attractions and activities were developed, although there was a lack of integration between the accommodation element and these activities in many cases.

The tourism strategy document, *Developing Sustainable Tourism 1993-97* (Bord Failte 1993), had identified 25 different rural tourism areas, whose criteria were based on natural and built resources of the area, commitment of the local community organisation, variety and distinctiveness of centres, and geographic balance. The National Tourist Board was aware that unrealistic expectations of rural tourism as an identified product had occurred in other countries, and it therefore identified these areas in order to provide a framework within which to concentrate activity.

There is an identified lack of training. Many of those who are involved in the business do not have business experience or formal training in skills such as management, customer service and marketing. *Teagasc*, LEADER+ companies, *Failte Ireland* and some destination groups have striven to combat this situation and provide advice and courses, encouraging participation through the provision of subsidies and certification.

Infrastructural shortcomings are recognised throughout rural Ireland. Internal transport is limited, impacting on both visitor and rural dweller and contributing to difficulty in gaining access to certain areas and for rural tourism practitioners attending meetings. These constraints need to be considered when both developing and marketing the rural tourism product.

Case Studies of the Co-operating Marketing Approach

In the early 1960s, farmhouse accommodation units were encouraged by *Bord Failte* (the National Tourist Board) to form a co-operative whose main objective would be to market the farmhouse accommodation sector. Thus Irish Farmhouse Holidays (IFH) was established, and has been in operation for almost 40 years. The organisation is limited by guarantee and its offices are situated in Limerick in the South West of Ireland. The organisation also depends greatly on voluntary contribution from its members as well as from paid staff. All accommodation is approved and fulfils minimum criteria for visitor accommodation.

CUSTOMER ENGAGEMENT

Customer engagement (CE) refers to the engagement of customers with one another, with a company or a brand. Unlike marketing terms such as positioning, customer engagement has not been traced to a single source. Customer engagement has been discussed widely online; hundreds of pages have been written, published, read and commented upon. Numerous high-profile conferences, seminars and roundtables have either had CE as a primary theme or included papers on the topic.

Customer engagement marketing places conversions into a longer term, more strategic context and is premised on the understanding that a simple focus on maximising conversions can, in some circumstances, decrease the likelihood of repeat conversions. CE aims at long-term engagement, encouraging customer loyalty and advocacy through word-of-mouth.

Online customer engagement is qualitatively different from offline engagement as the nature of the customer's interactions with a brand, company and other customers differ on the internet. Discussion forums or blogs, for example, are spaces where people can communicate and socialise in ways that cannot be replicated by any offline interactive medium. Customer Engagement marketing efforts that aim to create, stimulate or influence customer behaviour differ from the offline, one-way, marketing communications that marketers are familiar with. Although customer advocacy, for example, has always been a goal for marketers, the rise of online user generated content can take advocacy to another level.

The concept and practice of online Customer Engagement enables organisations to respond to the fundamental changes in customer behaviour that the internet has brought about, as well as to the increasing ineffectiveness of the traditional 'interrupt and repeat', broadcast model of advertising. Due to the fragmentation and specialisation of media and audiences, as well as the proliferation of community- and user generated content, businesses are increasingly losing the power to dictate the communications agenda. Simultaneously, lower switching costs, the geographical widening of the market and the vast choice of content, services and products available online have weakened customer loyalty.

So today, leveraging customer contributions is an important source of competitive advantage – whether through advertising, user generated product reviews, customer service FAQs, forums where consumers can socialise with one another or contribute to product development.

Amazon recently re-branded into 'serving the world's largest engaged online community', the World Federation of Advertisers (WFA) has created a 'Blueprint for Consumer-Centric Holistic Measurement' and the Association of National Advertisers (ANA), American Association of Advertising Agencies (AAAA) and the

Advertising Research Foundation (ARF), have put together the 'Engagement Steering Committee' to work on the customer engagement metric. Nielsen Media Research, IAG Research and Simmons Research are also all in the process of developing a CE definition and metric.

Online customer engagement refers to:

1. A **social phenomenon** enabled by the wide adoption of the internet in the late 1990s and taking off with the technical developments in connection speed (broadband) in the decade that followed. Online CE is qualitatively different from the engagement of consumers offline.
2. The behaviour of customers that engage in online communities revolving, directly or indirectly, around product categories (cycling, sailing) and other consumption topics. It details the process that leads to a customer's positive engagement with the company or offering, as well as the behaviours associated with different degrees of customer engagement.
3. **Marketing practices** that aim to create, stimulate or influence CE behaviour. Although CE-marketing efforts must be consistent both online and offline, the internet is the basis of CE-marketing.
4. **Metrics** that measure the effectiveness of the marketing practices which seek to create, stimulate or influence CE behaviour.

Customer engagement can also refer to the stages consumers travel through as they interact with a particular brand. This Customer Engagement Cycle, or Customer Journey, has been described using a myriad of terms but most often consists of 5 different stages: Awareness, Consideration, Inquiry, Purchase and Retention. Marketers employ Connection Strategy to speak to would-be customers at each stage, with media that addresses their particular needs and interests. When conducting Search Engine Marketing & Search Engine Optimization, or placing advertisements, marketers must devise media and/or keywords and phrases that encourage customer flow through the Customer Engagement Cycle, towards Purchase.

Because the various definitions often focus on entirely different aspects of CE, they are not in every case competing definitions but, rather, illuminate CE from different perspectives. Eric Peterson's definition for example frames CE as a metric: "Engagement is an estimate of the degree and depth of visitor interaction against a clearly defined set of goals."

At the moment the ARF, World Federation of Advertisers, Nielsen Media Research, IAG Research and Simmons Research are in the process of developing a definition and a metric for CE.

NEED FOR CUSTOMER ENGAGEMENT

CE-marketing is necessitated by a combination of social, technological and market developments:

Businesses are losing the power to dictate the communications agenda: The effectiveness of the traditional 'interrupt and repeat' model of advertising is decreasing. In August 2006, McKinsey & Co published a report which said that by 2010 traditional TV advertising will only be one-third as effective as it was in 1990. This is due to:

- Customer audiences are smaller and specialist: The fragmentation of media and audiences and the accompanying reduction of audience size have reduced the effectiveness of the traditional top-down, mass, 'interrupt and repeat' advertising model. The adoption of new media. Forrester Research's North American Consumer Technology Adoption Study shows people in the 18-26 age group spending more time online than watching TV.
- Customer audiences are also broadcasters: A company's position is no longer just inside consumers' minds. As they increasingly speak their minds with the power for circulation and permanence of CGM, businesses lose the power of shouting over everyone else. Instead of trying to

position a product using a couple of static messages that will themselves become the subject of conversation amongst a target market that has already discussed, positioned and rated the product, companies must join in. This also means that consumers can now choose not only when and how but, also, if they will engage with marketing communications; they can rely on CGM. In addition new media themselves provide consumers with more control over their advertising consumption.

Decreasing brand loyalty: The lowering of entry barriers (such as the need for a sales force, access to channels and physical assets) and the geographical widening of the market due to the internet have brought about increasing competition. In combination with lower switching costs, easier access to information about products and suppliers and increased choice customer loyalty is hard to achieve.

The increasing ineffectiveness of TV advertising due to the shift of consumer attention to the internet, the ability, within new media, to control advertising consumption and the decrease in audience size is bringing about a progressive shift of advertising spending online.

The proliferation of media that provide consumers with more control over their advertising consumption (subscription-based digital radio and TV for example) and the simultaneous decrease of faith in advertising and increase of faith in peers point to the need for communications that the customer will desire to engage with. Stimulating a consumer's engagement with a brand is the only way to increase brand loyalty and, therefore, "the best measure of current and future performance".

CE is the solution that marketers have devised in order to come to terms with the social, technological and market developments outlined above. In a nutshell, it is the attempt to create an engaging dialogue with target consumers and stimulate their engagement with the brand. Although this must take place consistently both on and off-line, the internet is the primary vehicle for doing so.

CE marketing begins with understanding the internal dynamics of these developments and, especially, the behaviour and engagement of consumers online. That way, business opportunities can be identified.

As Max Kalehoff suggests, consumer-generated media should play a massive role in our understanding and modelling of engagement. The control Web 2.0 consumers have gained must, and will be, quantified through 'old school' marketing performance metrics.

AS A SOCIAL PHENOMENON

Online inter-customer engagement is a recent social phenomenon that came about through the wide diffusion and adoption of the internet in western societies during the late 1990s. Although offline CE predates online CE, the latter is a qualitatively different social phenomenon unlike any offline CE that social theorists or marketers are familiar with.

People also engage online in communities that do not necessarily revolve around a particular product, but serve as meeting or networking places, for instance on MySpace. The people in one's MySpace friend's list do not necessarily all share a single consumption habit, although they often do.

People's online engagement with one another has brought about both the empowerment of consumers and the opportunity for businesses to engage with their target customers online.

AS CONSUMER BEHAVIOUR

CE behaviour became prominent with the advent of the social phenomenon of online CE. Creating and stimulating customer engagement behaviour has recently become an explicit aim of both profit and non-profit organisations in the belief that engaging target customers to a high degree is conducive to furthering business objectives.

Shevlin's definition of CE is well suited to understanding the process that leads to an engaged customer. In its adaptation by Richard Sedley the key word is 'investment'.

"Repeated interactions that strengthen the emotional, psychological or physical investment a customer has in a brand."

A customer's degree of engagement with a company lies in a continuum that represents the strength of his investment in that company. Positive experiences with the company strengthen that investment and move the customer down the line of engagement.

What is important in measuring degrees of involvement is the ability of defining and quantifying the stages on the continuum. One popular suggestion is a four-level model adapted from Kirkpatrick's Levels:

1. **Click** - A reader arrived (current metric)
2. **Consume** - A reader read the content
3. **Understood** - A reader understood the content and remembers it
4. **Applied** - A reader applies the content in another venue

Concerns have, however, been expressed as regards the measurability of stages three and four. Another popular suggestion is Ghuneim's typology of engagement.

The following consumer typology according to degree of engagement fits well to Ghuenim's continuum

- **Creators** (smallest group)
- **Critics**
- **Collectors**
- **Couch Potatoes** (largest group)

Engagement is a holistic characterisation of a consumer's behaviour, encompassing a host of sub-aspects of behaviour such as loyalty, satisfaction, involvement, Word of Mouth advertising, complaining and more.

- **Satisfaction**: Satisfaction is simply the foundation, and the minimum requirement, for a continuing relationship with customers. Engagement extends beyond mere satisfaction.
- **Loyalty - Retention**: Highly engaged consumers are more loyal. Increasing the engagement of target customers increases the rate of customer retention.
- **Word of Mouth advertising - advocacy**: Highly engaged customers are more likely to engage in free (for the company), credible (for their audience) Word of Mouth advertising. This can drive new customer acquisition and can have viral effects.
- **Awareness - Effectiveness of communications**: When customers are exposed to communication from a company that they are highly engaged with, they tend to actively elaborate on its central idea. This brings about high degrees of central processing and recall.
- **Filtering**: Consumers filter, categorise and rate the market from head to tail, creating multiple, overlapping folksonomies through tagging, reviewing, rating and recommending.
- **Complaint-behaviour**: Highly engaged customers are less likely to complain to other current or potential customers, but will address the company directly instead.
- **Marketing intelligence**: Highly engaged customers can give valuable recommendations for improving quality of offering.

The behavioural outcomes of an engaged consumer is what links CE to profits. From this point of view,

"CE is the best measure of current and future performance; an engaged relationship is probably the only guarantee for a return on your organisation's or your clients' objectives." Simply attaining a high level of customer satisfaction does not seem to guarantee the customer's business. 60% to 80% of customers who defect to a competitor said they were satisfied or very satisfied on the survey just prior to their defection.

The main difference between traditional and customer engagement marketing is marked by these shifts:

- From 'reach or awareness focused' marketing communications and their metrics (GRP or pageview) towards more targeted and customised interactions that prompt the consumer to engage with and act on the content from the outset.
- From absolute distinctions and barriers between an organisation and its target customers towards the participation of consumers in product development, customer service and other aspects of the brand experience.
- From one-way, top-down, formal B2C and B2E interaction to continuing, dialogic, decentralised and personalised communications initiated by either party.

Specific marketing practices involve:

- **Encouraging collaborative filtering**: Google, Amazon, iTunes, Yahoo LAUNCHcast, Netflix, and Rhapsody encourage their consumers to filter, categorise and rate; that is, to market their products. They realise consumers are not only much more adept at creating highly-targeted taxonomies (folksonomies) given that they are more adept at delineating the segment they themselves constitute, but, also, that they are willing to do so for free. And to the extent they cannot, they do it for them. If enough people like the band Groove Armada as well as the band The Crystal Method, there may well be a stylistic connection between them, despite the fact that one's categorised as 'downtempo' and the other 'beats and breaks'. Such strong associations tell Yahoo! to put the two on the same playlist more often, and if the positive ratings continue to come in, that connection is reinforced. (Anderson 2006:101) Amazon does the same with their 'customers who bought this item also bought...' recommendations.

- **Community development**: Helping target customers develop their own communities or create new ones.
- **Community participation**: Consumers do not filter and rate companies and their offerings within company websites only. Being able, with little effort, cost or technical skills, to create their own online localities, a large percentage of the filtering and rating takes place in non-sponsored, online spaces. Organisations must go and meet their target customers at their favoured online hangouts to not only listen but also participate in the dialogue.
- **Help consumers engage with one another**: Give them content (viral podcasting, videocasting, games, v-cards etc) they can use to engage with one another.
- **Solicitation of user generated content**: Engage them directly or indirectly with your product by giving them the means or incentive to create user generated content.
- **Customer self-service**: Help them create a customer service FAQ in wiki or blog format. Create a blog where technical support staff and customers can communicate directly.
- **Product co-development**: Create a blog where product developers and consumers can communicate directly.

CUSTOMER ENGAGEMENT AS A METRIC

All marketing practices, including Internet Marketing include measuring the effectiveness of various media along the Customer Engagement Cycle, as consumers travel from awareness to Purchase. Often the use of CVP Analysis factors into strategy decisions, including budgets and media placement.

The CE metric is useful for:

a) Planning:

- Identify where CE-marketing efforts should take place; which of the communities that the target customers participate in are the most engaging?

- Specify the way in which target customers engage, or want to engage, with the company or offering.

b) Measuring Effectiveness: Measure how successful CE-marketing efforts have been at engaging target customers.

The importance of CE as a marketing metric is reflected in ARF's statement:

"The industry is moving toward customer engagement with marketing communications as the 21st century metric of marketing efficiency and effectiveness."

ARF envisages CE exclusively as a metric of engagement with communication, but it is not necessary to distinguish between engaging with the communication and with the product since CE behaviour deals with, and is influenced by, involvement with both.

Eric Peterson's definition also frames CE as a metric:

"Engagement is an estimate of the degree and depth of visitor interaction on the site against a clearly defined set of goals."

In order to be operational, CE-metrics must be combined with psychodemographics. It is not enough to know that a website has 500 highly engaged members, for instance; it is imperative to know what percentage are members of the company's target market. As a metric for effectiveness, Scott Karp suggests, CE is the solution to the same intractable problems that have long been a struggle for old media: how to prove value.

The CE-metric is synthetic and integrates a number of variables. The World Federation of Advertisers calls it 'consumer-centric holistic measurement'. The following items have all been proposed as components of a CE-metric:

Root metrics

- Duration of visit
- Frequency of visit (returning to the site directly – through a URL or bookmark - or indirectly).
- % repeat visits

- Recency of visit
- Depth of visit (% of site visited)
- Click-through rate
- Sales
- Lifetime value

Action Metrics

- RSS feed subscriptions
- Bookmarks, tags, ratings
- Viewing of high-value or medium-value content (as valued from the organisation's point-of-view). 'Depth' of visit can be combined with this variable.
- Inquiries
- Providing personal information
- Downloads
- Content resyndication
- Customer reviews
- Comments: their quality is another indicator of the degree of engagement.
- Ratio between posts and comments plus trackbacks.

In selecting the components of a CE-metric, the following issues must be resolved:

- **Flexible metric vs. Industry standard**: According to some, CE "measurement has never been one size fits-all" but should vary according to industry, organisation, business goal etc. On the other hand, corporate clients and even agencies also desire some type of solid index. Internal metrics could, perhaps, be developed in addition to a comparative, industry-wide one. Other exponents of a flexible CE-metric include Bill Gassman in his comments to 'How do you calculate engagement? Part I'. Eric Peterson shares Gassman's views.

- **Relative weighting**: The relative weighting associated with each CE-component in an algorithm. For instance, is subscribing to RSS more important than contributing a comment? If yes how much more important exactly? Relative weighting links up with the issue of flexible vs. standardised metrics: Is the relative weighting going to be solid – as will be required if the CE-metric is to be standardised – or is it going to differ depending on the industry, organisation, business goals etc?
- **Component measurability**: Most of the components of a CE-metric face problems of measurement. Duration of visit for example suffers from (a) failing to capture the most engaged users who like to peruse RSS feeds; (b) inaccuracy arising from leaving a tab open during breaks, stopping to converse with co-workers, etc.
- **Length of measurement**: For how long must the various CE components be measured if CE is to reflect loyalty rather than short-term, faddish engagement?

10 FARM TOURISM COOPERATION

There is a large tourism industry in U.S that provides millions of international and domestic tourists. The country is the homeland for natural wonders, historical landmarks, cities, and gambling spots. People in US seek for comparable attractions in addition to the amusement and vacation areas.There are several alternatives for farmers and their organizations to get engaged with tourism. For instance, farmers can – next to their agricultural activities - provide accommodation or excursions. In this case the farmer is transformed into a rural tourism entrepreneur. Another option is that farmers deliver their products – food, fruits, crafts and curios - to the tourism economy. In this case, farmers are suppliers of goods to the tourism sector, an activity much closer to their original core business.

A distinguishing feature of rural tourism is to give the visitor a personalized experience, a taste of the physical, cultural and human environment of the countryside and as far as possible allow them to participate in activities, lifestyles and traditions of local communities .

Low involvement of farmer organizations : various factors and actors involved

Entering new non-farm sectors is often accompanied with barriers and patterns of inequality. In many developing countries the role of rural member based organizations in tourism development has yet to be recognized.

The low involvement of farmer organizations (FOs : rural producer organization, cooperatives, rural women organization) relates to their unawareness about the potential of rural tourism. Secondly, a lack of resources, experience and knowledge and the inability to harvest those, restrain FOs from accessing the tourism industry .

Thirdly, a lack of capitalization of experiences and documentation of successful models of cooperative tourism restrain FOs as well as those supporting them in their efforts to diversify.

The low participation of FOs in rural tourism is not only due to reasons related to the FOs itself. In general, direct support to FOs has long been and still is a neglected aspect in development cooperation. Furthermore, tourism stakeholders didn't consider FOs to be optional partners in tourism development. The fact that many farmers are geographically isolated from tourist areas and have little negotiation power, are other factors explaining the low involvement.

However when farmers are organized in organizations, they increase their political or commercial voice and possibilities to link with and opening up sectors unfamiliar to them.

Farmer organizations : key actors that need more attention for tourism development

However, over the last decade the recognition of FOs as partners in tourism development is growing. Additional to that tendency, FOs in developing counties are increasingly aware of the opportunities rural tourism can offer them.

Besides, creating additional income and employment, tourism development may improve the social well being in rural areas in a broad sense, for example by stimulating improvements in infrastructure, sanitary and electricity networks. Various Dutch development organizations such as Netherlands Development Organization (SNV), ICCO, Agriterra and Solidaridad are – each with their own strategy and practices - facilitating the creation of linkages between FOs and tourism, which were lacking before.

Although tourism development with FOs goes along with its challenges, there are several reasons advocating for increased inclusion of. Through the broad network and social structures that FOs already have throughout a region, they make the countryside better accessible for tourism developments. It places them in the position to uncover interesting locations as well as to identify suitable rural entrepreneurs. Tour operators don't have such links.

By working with FOs, tourism development in rural areas, will benefit not only individuals, but can become advantageous for a whole community. Additionally, it can contribute to financial sustainability of FOs. Finally, farmers can offer a unique authentic product to tourists ; the countryside, their way of living and their products. Tourists become are becoming increasingly interested in authentic and of-the-beaten-track experiences.

Agriterra and tourism : point of view of an NGO supporting FOs

Since 2005, rural tourism is embraced within Agriterra as a solution for economic diversification, poverty reduction and maintenance of local know-how, cultural life and heritage.

Currently ten partner organizations (Latin America, Asia and Africa) have started an agrotourism initiative. Some initiatives are already receiving tourists, others are still implementing. Examples of agritourism products developed by Agriterra partners are overnight stays in home stays or community lodges or tours (coffee or tea tour).

Until now Agriterra has most experience in supporting FOs in developing rural tourism products. Less experience is developed in integrating rural producers within tourism sector through so-called 'backward linkages' (connection between an industry and its suppliers) : farmers supply the tourism sector (hotels, restaurants) with their goods. Construction of such links is complex, but investment, training and education needs are considerable lower. Agriterra offers several services to FOs who are interested in tourism.

The tourism program of Agriterra aims to be outstanding in its focus on FOs and a businesslike approach. This business like approach is reflected in various aspects.

First, by stimulating to include market partners from the start. Tour operators can be involved in the identification of a location as well as in product development. What product will be most feasible and potential at a certain spot ? Secondly, a strong focus on business planning is stimulated. Furthermore much attention is paid on marketing, whereas marketing appears to be one of the main challenges.

Fourth, when a business plan appears to have potential, the farmers involved need to invest themselves in the venture in order to create commitment and stimulate an entrepreneurial attitude, that is, to take in account the professional and economic condition in order to develop appropriate and not to risky activities.

Preferably a micro-finance institute, bank or credit agency is involved. Because tourism is such a different sector for many farmers, intensive precaution in guidance is needed in order to develop a successful tourism initiative and to prevent farmers from bad experiences. When a FO seeks to start an initiative, from agriterra's point of view, the organization needs to present genuine interest for enrolling in tourism and have the capacity to do so.

Challenges : tourism activities that generate incomes for farmers

Although rural tourism development can certainly contribute to economic development in rural areas, it isn't a panacea for poverty reduction. When potential for rural tourism development appears to be present, success of the initiative depends on many aspects, such as product quality, the capacity of the organization, marketing and location of the venture.

Furthermore, the nature of the tourism industry is opportunistic, unpredictable and seasonal, therefore rural tourism needs to be approached as something additional to the agricultural activities of farmers. To become competitive, a FO needs to develop a commercial viable product, which is challenging. Adequate product development needs structural guidance from tourism professionals in order to comply with Western tourism standards.

Furthermore intensive training of the people involved – tour guides, cooks, home stay owners, etc – in the various aspects of tourism management and reception is crucial, but often lacking. In turn, marketing and promotion of the tourism initiative appears to be one of the bottlenecks.

Another challenge is obtaining insight in the level of returns compared to its investments. Only few cost-benefits studies have been done in this sector. Since FOs are rather new actors in rural tourism, there isn't an extensive body of knowledge generated this arena. Agriterra aims to contribute in capitalizing best practices and successful models of cooperative tourism for integrating FOs in the tourism sector.

A scenic route that connects the continental United States with Alaska, the Alaska Highway attracts many travelers each year. Also known as the Alcan Highway, the road begins in Dawson Creek, British Columbia, ends in Delta Junction, Alaska and runs more than 1,500 miles. It remains an adventure road, especially in the wintertime when temperatures drop far below freezing. The topography of the road at times presents challenges for tourists, but every year they continue to travel the highway in increasing numbers.

The Alcan Highway did not begin as a tourist route, but instead as a military operation. Completed in 1943, construction commenced during World War II because of the need for an emergency route between Alaska and the continental United States. Paying all the costs of the road's construction, the U.S. turned over control of the Canadian portion of the road six months after the end of the war, while retaining control of the section in Alaska.

In the years immediately after construction, a traveler had to apply for a special military permit to travel the Alaska Highway. It opened up to the general public in 1948, but remained a dangerous road to travel. Many portions of the road remained unpaved, but tourism still grew steadily. Lodges and government-run campgrounds opened up all over the highway, along with gas stations, garages and cafes.

While the historic mileposts no longer give an accurate distance due to the shortening and straightening out of the highway in recent years, they still mark important locations for both tourists and locals. Dawson Creek, British Columbia, the southern end of the Alaska Highway, remains a popular historic spot. Delta Junction, Alaska marks the historic northern end of the highway. Contact Creek, the meeting point of the two teams working to build the highway from north to south, also bears historic significance.

Most of the Alcan Highway winds through wilderness and undeveloped land, and largely remains a scenic route. Travelers see the beauty of the Yukon wilderness firsthand. Tourists flock to the area for fishing, hunting and other outdoor sports. Wonowon, British Columbia, located alongside the highway, leads to rivers, mountains and other natural wonders. Another destination, the Tetsa River Regional Park, located in the foothills of the Rocky Mountains, remains a popular area for nature lovers along the highway.

For tourists who love animals, the observation of a wide variety of wildlife is possible. Deer and moose commonly graze alongside the Alcan Highway and drivers must take care to avoid them.

The Tetlin National Wildlife Refuge enjoys popularity among tourists for its rich variety of animal and plant life. Located in Alaska, it runs adjacent to the Alaska Highway for more than 60 miles. Nature lovers can drop by the Visitor's Center to learn more about the wildlife, or go camping out in the wilderness.

In developing country like India, farm tourism is in an initial phase. Take the case of Haryana state. Haryana, known for introducing 'Highway tourism' for the first time in the country, is now paying attention to promote 'farm tourism' to enable domestic and foreign tourists.The concept of farm tourism is a part of village tourism and seeks to take the modern man back to his roots though at a price. The concept was launched by the Haryana tourism corporation in the year 2003.In this novel concept of farm tourism, the state tourism department acts as facilitator and promoter of package tours to farm houses. The owners of the farm houses act as guide and host and provide boarding, lodging, food and other facilities to the tourists.

The Haryana tourism corporation provides professional guidance and link services to farm house owners. Village tourism has brought new job opportunities for local youth. Village tourism has contributed towards reinstating the charm of rural life style restoring pride among the villagers. It provides opportunities to the farmers to show their achievements to the outsiders and take pride in it. The concept has not only generated employment but has also imparted a sense of dignity among the villagers.

It is going to play a vital role in bridging the gap between rural and urban India cultural exchange process. The stress of urban lifestyles has led to growing interest in this concept. There are other factors, which are shifting the trend towards farm tourism like increasing levels of awareness, growing interest in heritage and culture and improved accessibility and environmental consciousness. The farm tourism has wide dimension of earning because this can yield additional income can be generated from agriculture practice and also there is no need of additional capital investment for business and operation can be done by full family involvement besides it provides them with...

FARMHOUSE

Farmhouse is a general term for the main house of a farm. It is a type of building or house which serves a residential purpose in a rural or agricultural setting. Most often, the surrounding environment will be a farm. These buildings are usually 2 stories, but early buildings were single story. Many farm houses are shaped like a T. The perpendicular section is referred to as the ell.

These several buildings tend to be more pragmatic than aesthetic, but often well-stocked or well-furnished in terms of food, insulation or in other aspects dealing with daily necessities. The supply of agricultural products from its environment tends to be a factor for this, as well as stressing the need for productivity and pragmatism in the survival of the farm. The farmhouse allows the farmers, workers and often their families to reside in proximity to their workplace—namely the farm in question. This allows the farmers and workers to arrive at the workplace earlier, increasing the productivity of the farm.

EUROPE

Germany

Historically there were three main types of German farmhouse, many of which still survive today. The Low German house or *Niedersachsenhaus* (Lower Saxony house) is found mainly on the North German Plain, but also in large parts of Holland. It is a large, unit structure with a large, sweeping roof supported by two to four rows of internal posts. The great gateway at the gable end opens into a large hall or *Deele*, with cattle stalls and barns to either side and living accommodation at the end.

The Middle German house may also be a single unit, but access is from the side and the roof is supported by the outside walls. Later this type of *mitteldeutsches Haus* was expanded to two or more buildings around a rectangular farmyard, often with a second storey. The South German house is found in southern Germany and has two main variants: the Swabian or Black Forest farmstead and the Bavarian farmstead.

Norway

Norwegian farmhouses used timber or logs and built using Scandinavian vernacular architecture. The first examples are traced back to the 13th century

United Kingdom

Lately, in the United Kingdom, "farmhouse" has come to be used to mean an expensive housing estate in the countryside, away from the city. In this modern extended use of the term, the farmhouse may or may not be related to an actual farm—frequently, in fact, "farmhouses" are not based around any actual farm. While farm produce sustained the traditional farmhouses, sustenance for the modern farmhouse is provided by outside resources.

These modern farmhouses are often a rural retreat for wealthy people who come to these places for vacation and rest, or to escape the atmosphere of the city. While many of these farmhouses have been handed down through generations, where originally farm produce could have been the main revenue source, other such farmhouses are being built new.

Canada

Canadian farmhouses were influenced by European settlers. In Quebec, the style varied from Gothic to Swiss. In Ontario, the farmhouses of the late 19th century was of Victorian influence. Earlier ones used clapboard and later variations had brick. Many had porches out front. A dirt road would lead to the nearest concession road.

As for out west, dwellings varied from single story wooden homesteads to straw huts. Wooden houses were built later as railroads allowed wood to be shipped from the Rockies (Alberta, BC) by 1915 they could be purchased as kits from Eaton's catalog. Canadian homes often differ from their American counterparts in that the porch is enclosed.

United States

Sometimes farmhouse may refer to a building design style, or a building's former purpose. This may occur when the farming area has been developed for other purposes, but the building itself still stands. Architectural styles vary, but very often they are of Cape Cod design. In general styles vary from region to region, but more often the style is simplistic so to serve the needs (and the budget) of the owners.

Sustainable Tourism Research

Sustainable tourism research is the cornerstone of a growing global initiative. Sustainable tourism development promises to provide more meaningful tourism experiences along with social and economic growth in undeveloped and disadvantaged nations and communities. Sustainable tourism research extends beyond the boundaries of tourism to include every facet of contemporary society.

Type

Eco-tourism promotes wilderness experiences.Sustainable tourism research focuses on a broad spectrum of sustainable development and management practices across tourism types and destinations. Sustainable development surrounding tourism includes infrastructure, building and business, along with environmental and cultural resources. Eco-tourism is sometimes used interchangeably with sustainable tourism but often refers specifically to tourism that focuses on cultural, environmental, educational and experiential travel.

Significance

Local stakeholders are critical in sustainable tourism research. Sustainable tourism research focuses on assessing current conditions, identifying critical stakeholders, tourism planning, implementation methods and methods for gathering and reviewing results data. Sustainable destination research locates successful case studies that can serve as models for the development of sustainable tourism initiatives. Sustainable tourism research focuses on available assets and current unsustainable practices and conditions.

Benefits

Sustainable tourism development builds economies. Sustainable tourism research reveals increased economic benefits from the development of sustainable tourism. Tourism receipts in developing nations increased from $50 billion in 1990 to $205 billion in 2005. Eco-tourists spend money directly in local economies, where it immediately benefits local stakeholders. Eco-tourists spend money across a broad spectrum within sustainable destinations and consume a variety of goods and services throughout their stay. The influx of eco-tourism dollars can lead to the creation of small businesses in struggling economies and increase local involvement in environmental and cultural preservation.

Effects

Sustainable tourism manages growth and development to preserve resources.Sustainable tourism research uncovers a range of potential positive and negative impacts to consider. Positive effects include economic growth, infrastructure development, preservation of natural and cultural resources and the potential to improve socioeconomic conditions in developing communities and nations. Negative impacts include potential degradation of natural and cultural resources resulting from unrestrained growth and development and the potential for clashes between local stakeholders, tourists and developers.

Potential

Rural tourism continues to grow as people seek to escape from crowded urban areas. Sustainable tourism research continues to expand beyond the boundaries of ecological, cultural and heritage sites to include the rising popularity of adventure tourism, rural and farm tourism and philanthropy tourism. Sustainable tourism development increasingly encompasses the larger community and promotes sustainable infrastructure, waste management and reduction, environmental protection, building standards, clean energy, clean water and sustainable business practices.

Local Community

A community is a group of interacting organisms sharing an environment. In human communities, intent, belief, resources, preferences, needs, risks, and a number of other conditions may be present and common, affecting the identity of the participants and their degree of cohesiveness. A community has been defined as a group of interacting people living in a common location.

The word is often used to refer to a group that is organized around common values and is attributed with social cohesion within a shared geographical location, generally in social units larger than a household. The word can also refer to the national community or global community. A sense of community refers to people's perception of interconnection and interdependence, shared responsibility, and common goals.

Rural tourism can be envisaged as contributing to economic and social development of local communities, by including tourism policies, as well as specific programmes and projects that aim at the reduction of poverty levels. Based on the analysis of a series of different county experiences, our paper emphasizes that, from the host community's point of view, essential goals of tourism development must include generating higher levels of income, creating new employment opportunities, and increasing foreign exchange flows.

Equally important, any such development must also protect the environment and especially the local culture, to which tourists are attracted in the first place. This is why the potential of rural tourism in local communities should be a central consideration in discussions on policies regarding poverty alleviation.

An associated challenge is how to ensure that the local communities retain their 'authentic' character to ensure sustainable long-term success without becoming too dependent on tourism but yet still benefit enough economically to make it worthwhile. Throughout the analysis, we find that tourism is a potent force that is intimately intertwined with rural issues throughout the world and has had a dramatic impact most notably in developing countries.

But, rural tourism, though a powerful tool for economic development and heritage sustainability, needs great care and sensitivity in planning, management and marketing to be socially as well as economically viable. It is suggested that tourism must not distort, but rather complement the local village economy, which is usually based on agri-rural production.

BENEFITS OF LOCAL COMMUNITY

Author Robert Putnam refers to the value which comes from social networks as social capital in his book "Bowling Alone: The collapse and Revival of American Community." He writes that social capital "makes an enormous difference in our lives", that "a society characterized by generalized reciprocity is more efficient that a distrustful society" and that economic sociologists have shown a minimized economic wealth if social capital is lacking.

Putnam reports that the first use of the social capital theory was by L. J. Hanifan, a practical reformer during the Progressive Era in the United States of America. The following description of social capital is a quote from L.J. Hanifan in Putnam's Book:

Those tangible substances count for most in the daily lives of people: namely good will, fellowship, sympathy, and social intercourse among individuals and families who make up a social unit.... The individual is helpless socially, if left to himself....

If he comes into contact with neighbor, and they with other neighbors, there will be an accumulation of social capital, which may immediately satisfy his social needs and which may bear a social potentiality sufficient to the substantial improvement of living conditions in the whole community. The community as a whole will benefit by the cooperation of all its parts, while the individual will find in his associations the advantages of the help, sympathy, and fellowship of his neighbors.

Employment

Putnam reported that many studies have shown that the highest predictor of job satisfaction is the presence of social connection in the workplace. He writes that "people with friends at work are happier at work." And that "social networks provide people with advice, a bonus, a promotion, and other strategic information, and letters of recommendation."

Community engagement has been proven to counteract the most negative attributes of poverty and a high amount of social capital has been shown to reduce crime.

Local Community and Health

"Social connectedness matters to our lives in the most profound way."

-Robert Putnam.

Robert Putnam reports, in the chapter *Health and Happiness* from his book *Bowling Alone*, that recent public research shows social connection impacts all areas of human health, this includes psychological and physical aspects of human health. Putnam say's "...beyond a doubt that social connectedness is one of the most powerful determinates of our well being." In particular it is face to face connections which have been show to have greater impacts then non-face to face relationships.

Specific health benefits of strong social relationships are a decrease in the likelihood of: seasonal viruses, heart attacks, strokes, cancer, depression, and premature death of all sorts.

COMMUNITY SUSTAINABILITY

Sustainability in community programs is the capacity of programs (services designed to meet the needs of community members) to continuously respond to community issues.

A sustained program maintains a focus consonant with its original goals and objectives, including the individuals, families, and communities it was originally intended to serve. Programs change regarding the breadth and depth of their programming. Some become aligned with other organizations and established institutions, whereas others maintain their independence. Understanding the community context in which programs serving the community function has an important influence on program sustainability and success.

Top Ten Reasons to Buy Local

According to Washington State's Sustain South Sound organization, the top ten reasons to buy local are:

1. Too strengthen local economy: Studies have shown that buying from an independent, locally owned business, significantly raises the number of times your money is used to make purchases from other local businesses, service providers and farms—continuing to strengthen the economic base of the community.
2. Increase jobs: Small local businesses are the largest employer nationally in the United Sates of America.
3. Encourage local prosperity: A growing body of economic research shows that in an increasingly homogenized world, entrepreneurs and skilled workers are more likely to invest and settle in communities that preserve their one-of-a-kind businesses and distinctive character.
4. Reduce environmental impact: Locally owned businesses can make more local purchases requiring less transportation and generally set up shop in town or city centers as opposed to developing on the fringe. This means contributing less to greenhouse gas emissions, sprawl, congestion, habitat loss and pollution.
5. Support community groups: Non-profit organizations receive an average 250% more support from smaller business owners than they do from large businesses.
6. Keep your community unique: Where we shop, where we eat and have fun—all of it makes our community home.
7. Get better service: Local businesses often hire people with a better understanding of the products they are selling and take more time to get to know customers.

8. Invest in community: Local businesses are owned by people who live in the community, are less likely to leave, and are more invested in the community's future.
9. Put your taxes to good use: Local businesses in town centers require comparatively little infrastructure investment and make more efficient use of public services as compared to nationally owned stores entering the community.
10. Buy what you want, not what someone wants you to buy: A marketplace of tens of thousands of small businesses is the best way to ensure innovation and low prices over the long-term. A multitude of small businesses, each selecting products based not on a national sales plan but on their own interests and the needs of their local customers, guarantees a much broader range of product choices.

ANDERSONVILLE STUDY

This compelling study, commissioned by the Andersonville Development Corporation, finds that locally owned businesses generate 70 percent more local economic impact per square foot than chain stores. The study's authors, Dan Houston and Matt Cunningham of Civic Economics, analyzed ten locally owned restaurants, retail stores, and service providers in the Andersonville neighborhood on Chicago's north side and compared them with ten national chains competing in the same categories.

They found that spending $100 at one of the neighborhood's independent businesses creates $68 in additional local economic activity, while spending $100 at a chain produces only $43 worth of local impact. They also found that the local businesses generated slightly more sales per square foot compared to the chains ($263 versus $243). Because chains funnel more of this revenue out of the local economy, the study concluded that, for every square foot of space occupied by a chain, the local economic impact is $105, compared to $179 for every square foot occupied by an independent business.

What role should rural economic development agencies play?

- As active listeners.
- As experts with a system to help locals organize their thoughts.
- As connective tissue between and among communities ready for collaboration.
- As a resource for solutions that have worked in other communities.
- As a source of grant possibilities to implement locally generated and supported projects that are part of a long-term planned outcome.

This is a tall order.

It is common, instead for "experts" to go into an area, assess the "needs" for a rural community to add a tourism component to their economic mix. They often leave without ever having talked to anyone other than city hall and the loudest mouth in town.

It is rare to find a small town in the US that doesn't have a "tourism study" gathering dust on a shelf somewhere.

I'm on a mission to discover agencies and organizations effectively filling the roles listed above.

Next week I'll be presenting at the British Columbia Rural Tourism Conference on how the Kansas Sampler Foundation helps rural communities.

The Kansas Sampler Foundation was formed in the mid 1990's after Executive Director and Kansas resident Marci Penner finished an extended trip through the Kansas countryside.

She observed that Kansas rural communities were rich with culture and history that was being largely overlooked by the locals. By looking without judging, she discovered local treasures in every small town.

Rural Culture Elements

She noted that every aspect of rural community and culture falls into one of eight categories, which she calls the 8 Rural Culture Elements.

Through the Kansas Sampler Foundation, she is working with volunteers from rural communities throughout Kansas to help them identify and inventory their own Rural Culture Elements.

This simple process is transforming communities.

They see their own assets with new eyes.

They begin to understand that they already have something to offer visitors looking for an authentic rural experience.

They have a context for new development. Knowing their Rural Culture Elements helps communities to see where outside grant assistance will help them preserve their local culture and enhance the economic benefit.

The Eight Rural Culture Elements have become so much a part of Kansas culture, a statewide contest has been going on to discover the Eight Wonders of Kansas Culture in time for their sesquicentennial celebration next year.

Explorer Tourism

In addition, the Kansas Sampler Foundation is helping rural communities market themselves to visitors who will appreciate them as they are. National Geographic Society calls them Geo-tourists.

- They are interested in local culture.
- They are curious about what is already there.
- They want their visit to be a part of sustaining that local culture rather than changing or destroying it.
- They are willing to "do dirt" to get to their destination. They shop at local stores and love to dine at local eateries.

The Kansas Sampler Foundation has started a Kansas based travel club for Explorers. Monthly newsletters and online forums keep Explorers in contact with group travel opportunities and individual discoveries throughout Kansas.

With rural communities having a ready tourism market through Explorer Tourism, the next obvious step was to encourage collaboration among towns. Collaboration, while a good idea, is difficult to implement among small towns for a host of reasons. (This needs to be covered in another post in the future.)

Besides featuring rural communities, it clusters all Rural Culture Elements within their eight categories. This makes it easier for Explorers to create travel itineraries to, for instance, visit all historic soda fountains or see all Kansas Geographic Wonders, or go on a quest to find the best chicken fried steak.

The Internet allows collaboration to happen around Rural Culture Elements through the ingenuity and creativity of the Explorer visitors themselves.

The Kansas Sampler Foundation's mission encompasses more that facilitating tourism. They're interested in every aspect of supporting and sustaining the viability of rural communities. They work along side the regional resource conservation and development organizations, the state tourism office and other economic development entities.

Tourists to Get High on Fresh Air

Image Caption: Spectacular views above Crans Montana

The creation of a new label could be a breath of fresh air for Swiss alpine resorts and their guests. More than a marketing ploy, the "pure air" claim will be backed by the findings of scientific studies proving the health benefits of high altitude holidays.

"Resorts are rediscovering fresh mountain air and its corresponding health benefits as an asset that can be marketed," says researcher Rafael Matos.

The air is more than fresh in Crans Montana, it's so cold and damp that I can literally see the words forming in front of Matos as we walk through the mountain resort.

Matos has been working on a three-year project run out of the University of Lausanne investigating the "scientific and cultural history of air as a component of alpine landscapes".

Despite the rather scholarly title, the results could have practical applications for alpine resorts.

Matos, who is the team member responsible for contemporary issues, says the eventual creation of a "pure air" label could be assigned to places like Crans Montana.

Turning Back the Clock

If this happens, resorts will be turning back the clock since the health benefits of high altitude holidays were first recognised in the 19th century, when people from across Europe afflicted with respiratory diseases, including tuberculosis, flocked to the Alps.

That was before the discovery of antibiotics, and an outbreak of a winter sports madness that transformed many alpine villages into ski resorts.

It also made the villages lose sight of their 19th century beginnings.

Austria was the first to rediscover the potential a few years ago when the university of Innsbruck published a study comparing the benefits of vacations in the mountains to holidaying at lower altitudes.

It found that people who holidayed at moderate altitudes (1,500-2,000m) had lower blood pressure and pulse rates, lost weight and slept better.

Key Factor

Following up on the study, Matos's group surveyed 1,000 tourists across the Alps who said the unpolluted mountain air was a key factor in choosing their destination – second only to the scenic beauty.

Some mountain resorts have been using this natural resource as a selling point, but not as aggressively as they could.

Matos says the chance of breathing rarefied air is even more important for the increasing numbers of Chinese, Russian and Indian tourists who are coming to the Swiss Alps to escape their smog-choked cities.

But he says a "pure air" label, if created, would come at a cost and Crans Montana, for example, would not qualify if the label existed today.

Traffic Plague

While the air quality on its ski slopes and hiking trails is rated among the best in the Swiss Alps, the resort centre is plagued by motorised traffic.

Matos says the authorities have to do more to reduce traffic congestion, especially over the Christmas period and in February – the height of the ski season - when the resort population increases tenfold.

"We can see it, hear it and even smell it," Matos says, speaking over the roar of cars.

"The majority of our guests still come by car because it's very accessible that way," admits director of tourism, Walter Loser.

Loser lays part of the blame on the mentality of Crans Montana's mostly French- and Italian-speaking guests who want the fresh air as much as anybody else, but refuse to give up the convenience of their cars when on holiday.

New Road

But Loser says Crans Montana has chosen to go down a different road.

As part of a government-funded pilot project to promote health and a healthy environment, the resort is implementing new measures to convince visitors to use the excellent public transport system.

It is turning parts of the centre into a pedestrian zone and is drastically reducing speed limits.

In the poll position for the "pure air" label, according to Matos, are Switzerland's nine car-free resorts including Zermatt, Saas Fee and Mürren.

But he says that even they have to do more to get visitors to take the train instead of driving to one of the giant car parks on the edge of the villages, where cars can be parked.

If it is introduced, a "pure air" label could win back tourists who have over the past couple of decades forsaken the Alps for relaxing beach holidays.

That would at the very least be good for the health of the Swiss tourist industry.

11 The Development of Tourism Businesses in Rural Communities

At its best, rural tourism combines the virtues of a slower pace of life, getting closer to nature and learning about agriculture, and experiencing authentic local cultures by living among local villagers for a short time. From its tea plantations to its tribal villages, Malaysia offers all of these things in a deep green tropical setting.

Rural tourism encompasses two broad types of travel interests. One is the opportunity to live near or in a relatively isolated rural village, enjoy the quiet life and experience truly authentic local culture. This takes the form of homestays in rural areas, particularly in the villages of the Orang Asli, a tribal group living mostly in the forests of central Peninsular Malaysia. Agritourism is rural tourism that focuses on agriculture, sometimes to the extent of living and working part time on a farm. Malaysia's version focuses on tropical fruits and tea plantations.

Homestay rural tourism in Malaysia routinely includes the opportunity to participate in local events such as weddings or festivals, explore the area's outdoor features such as caves full of giant fruit bats, take part in craft demonstrations, and learn a little bit about local agricultural practices. However, as the patron is usually one of just a few tourists in the area, these activities are more intimate than is often the case with organized day tours.

HOME BUSINESS IDEAS FOR RURAL AREAS

Working from home in a rural area allows parents to earn an income while spending more time involved with their children and enjoying the great outdoors. Utilizing the natural surroundings can allow country residents to create unique gift, beauty, and edible items to sell at both craft shows and online. Hosts of websites exist for crafters and artisans to sell their wares online to a worldwide audience.

Open a greenhouse as a rural home-based business.

Rural living often means owning multiple acres of land, and perhaps even a pond. Renting space for camping or building cabins to earn larger rental rates will generate year-round income. Eco-tourism is a growing trend across the country and can earn a year-round income for camping providers.

Camping and fishing businesses are successful rural investments.

Gardening can earn those with a green thumb an excellent work-from-home income. Selling fresh garden produce as well as canned homegrown produce during the winter months can entice travelers and locals alike to a roadside fruit and vegetable stand. Marketing the products online and offering shipment of the canned food can increase potential income.

Developing a personalized label on the computer to add to the Mason jars before shipment adds a down-home touch to the product. Opening a greenhouse next to the home is another excellent example of a rural business idea. Free greenhouse plans can be found online and are relatively inexpensive to construct.

The greenhouse can provide seeds to area farmers and gardeners, as well as perennial and annual flowers and bulbs. Setting up a website to promote and sell the greenhouse items increases the exposure and potential revenue for the home-based business.Making candles and soap requires only a small space in the home and ties in well with countryside visitors and eco-travelers. Organic and scented recipes for both candles and soap can be found online at no cost.

Open a Miniature Golf Course or Petting Zoo

Opening a tourist or family friendly low-budget attraction offers an interactive home-based business in rural America. A miniature golf course or petting zoo can tie in to the use of unused acreage on rural property while generating extra income. Promoting the rural attraction on tourism websites and with regional newspapers will bring paying customers from outside the local area. Offering the opportunity to ride a pony or milk a cow would make the experience even more interesting for urban visitors.

Organized Day Tours

Agriculture-focused tourism ranges from organized day tours that scratch the surface of how tea or fruits are grown, harvested and processed, to multi-night stays on a plantation or farm. The latter includes hands-on, part-time labor. Depending on the program and time of year, patrons might find themselves planting a jackfruit tree or learning how and when to pick the buds from a tea bush.

In addition to the educational and other personal benefits to the patrons of rural tourism, this form of travel also offers some benefits to Malaysia. Homestays in rural areas puts hard capital directly into the hands of poorer rural communities. Homestays in Orang Asli villages in particular help draw attention to the plight of these people, who are sometimes harassed by the government with the aim of assimilating them into Malay Muslim culture. Through judicious research and selection, an agritourism trip can be used to promote sustainable agricultural practices in Malaysia.

The Malaysian Agriculture Research and Development Institute (MARDI) offers agri-tourism tours and packages amid the tea plantations of the Cameron Highlands and at a fruit farm in Langkawi. The Desaru Fruit Farm offers its own agritourism packages in the state of Johor. Sabah Tea in Borneo is also in the agritourism business. Homestays are available throughout both

Peninsular Malaysia and Malaysian Borneo, and it also is possible to visit Orang Asli villages independently in national parks like Taman Negara.

Travel into the rural areas of Malaysia exposes tourists to greater health risks than staying in the cities or at a beach resort. The Centers for Disease Control specifically recommends vaccinations against typhoid, Japanese encephalitis and rabies; a prescription for anti-malarial medication; and the use of insect repellents to ward off other insect-borne diseases like dengue fever for those venturing into rural areas of Malaysia.

For the past several years, interest in rural tourism development has grown. And because of the renewed interest in America's rural communities, it should continue to grow. This nation has discovered that approximately 96 percent of its population lives on four percent of its land, which means that four percent of U.S. citizens are spread out over 96 percent of our landmass.

As such, although there are many people who have always been interested in rural research, many of the problems associated with rural communities have become popular over the past few years and are being researched and discussed by both academics and community leaders.

One of the most popular issues is rural community development and the use of tourism as a tool for that development. There is a wealth of information about rural tourism including economic analysis of tourism, its impacts, and its effect on people. In addition, there has been a great deal published that concerns those various topics.

In fact, in the September 1993 issue of Parks & Recreation, Brian Hill outlined the opportunities and challenges presented by rural tourism. Rural tourism has grown a great deal since his article, as has the research on the problems and challenges of tourism. However, many of the factors and challenges he talked about in 1993 are still prevalent today.

The intent of this article is to discuss a new issue (not discussed by Hill) in rural tourism development that of the developmental processes it. One of the greatest challenges to rural tourism has actually been produced by the popularity and growth of tourism in rural communities. Because tourism is so popular, rural community leaders are racing to establish tourism in their communitics, yet they often lack the understanding of the tourism development process that makes it difficult to generate tourism.

If rural leaders do not understand how tourism begins or what processes are involved with tourism, they cannot possibly understand or deal with the resulting impacts of tourism in their community.

SEARCHING FOR ECONOMIC DEVELOPMENT

Rural communities, just like urban areas, are constantly searching for economic development opportunities. Recently, as federal and state governments have curtailed funding to rural communities, economic development has become vitally important. As rural leaders search for economic development opportunities, one particular type of development that has become very attractive is tourism.

Tourism is a viable method of development because it is economically feasible, relatively clean (does not rely on manufacturing), enhances the recreation opportunities in a community, and is a method of economic advancement and development that can be undertaken by the residents and leaders of a rural community.

Rural tourism development is attractive because of the perception that it is a clean and economical way to generate revenue. The economics of tourism are such that very often the revenue from tourism is generated by tourists (non-natives or non-residents of a community.) Visitors generate revenue as they spend money and pay tourism-dedicated taxes. For example, many communities have an innkeeper's tax (the most popular type of tourism-dedicated tax) on hotel and motel rooms.

Typically an innkeeper's tax (bed tax) is incurred by visitors to the community, not residents of the community. Hence, the tax is popular because it generates revenue without taxing the residents, and the revenue is usually dedicated to tourism development.

Thus, a community can often develop tourism without taxing the residents of the community, which makes tourism attractive not only to the leaders of the community but to the residents, as well. There is also a variety of other taxes that creates revenue from tourism; and most tax the visitors, not the residents. These include tourism-dedicated food and beverage tax and special licensing taxes.

The development of tourism in a rural community is perceived as a "dean" industry. For many years, rural communities were involved in a practice referred to as "buffalo hunting." Buffalo hunting involves rural leaders developing their communities by attracting companies and their manufacturing plants. Companies were offered tax concessions and cheap land as an attraction.

However, the combination of tax concessions and the lack of a labor pool and community infrastructure often resulted in a net loss for a community and a very noisy, dirty manufacturing plant. Thus, attracting manufacturing and new business proved to be a difficult task, one that often affected a community's quality of life.

Rural leaders discovered they could develop tourism without the tax concessions, the large labor pool, and the large, ugly manufacturing plant; and often, tourism development improves the quality of life. Therefore, the development of tourism is more effective — and cleaner— than attempting to attract manufacturing plants. Because of the opportunities presented by tourism development, there is no longer the need to scramble to bring a manufacturing company to a community.

In addition to creating jobs and revenue, rural tourism often increases the recreational opportunities in the community. For example, attractions are created or built (built tourism) to attract tourists, but at the same time, residents of the community benefit from using them. Sometimes the influx of tourists results in new recreational opportunities and improvements to parks, instances that are not often found in a rural community.

Tourism also frequently enhances the spectrum of recreational opportunities in a rural community. For example, hotels or motels may build attractions for tourists that can also be used by the residents of the community.

Perhaps the most attractive thing about developing tourism in a rural community is that the leaders and residents of the community can foster pride and establish responsibility for the process of development. That is, the community can utilize local resources as well as local organizations to create tourism.

Tourism is an opportunity that residents can create from within the community; it does not have to rely on out-of-state businesses or companies. New research has shown that this idea of development within the community has begun to take root. It is something that a rural community can do by itself with assistance from — not reliance on — outside sources.

Disadvantages to Rural Communities

Of course, rural tourism development does not come without a price. While it may improve revenue, quality of life, and recreational opportunities, there are reasons to be concerned about the social, cultural, and environmental impacts of tourism on a rural community. Many rural leaders and residents have discovered (often by surprise) that encouraging large numbers of visitors to come to a small community often creates problems.

The social and cultural problems can be numerous. Socially, the small rural community atmosphere dissipates quickly. Neighbors may not be able to stand at their white picket fence and chat with one another because there is a crowd of tourists on the street. In fact, it is not unusual for residents of a rural community that features popular tourism attractions to become unhappy when they find that at peak tourism times a simple five-minute trip to the post office can become a two-hour ordeal.

In addition, residents of a rural community often do not have the same perception of tourism as does the tourist. Tourists flock to rural communities to soak up the town's "down to earth," friendly quality, while residents often view tourists as outsiders.

As tourism becomes popular, the culture of a rural community can also change rapidly. People tend to perceive a rural community as a place where children play on safe streets, where there is little or no crime, and where everyone welcomes you to their house. In many rural communities where tourism has developed, that perception is no longer true. The hidden side of rural tourism development (one not often discussed) includes crime and other serious societal problems that are imported to a rural community, problems that can radically alter a community's culture.

Research has also illustrated that rural tourism development can create its share of environmental problems. The allure of a rural community is often its quiet, unaffected beauty and "quaint" charm. The advent of tourism creates the need for infrastructure, which often results in litter, noise, and air pollution in addition to other environmental problems. For example, the influx of tourists to Brown County, Indiana, has granted Brown County State Park the dubious distinction of being one of the most visited state parks in the nation.

As a result, the park, known for its unique environmental beauty, now often suffers from overcrowding and a fragile ecosystem. Raccoon State Recreation Area, located in west central Indiana, is a very popular recreation area, but because of overcrowding, it is often forced to close its gates to tourists.

Tourism development may also cause infrastructure-related problems for a community. The demand for amenities — hotels, restaurants, and even public restrooms — places a strain upon the infrastructure resources of a rural community. Rural communities often lack the resources to erect new buildings, create new sewer systems, or supply police and fire services.

The influx of tourists forces a rural community to pave roads, provide better police and fire protection, keep the streets clean, and maintain a stressed infrastructure. In order to maintain such infrastructure, a small rural community needs money, a resource that is oftentimes unavailable to rural community governments.

Thus, rural tourism development, a popular method of economic development, one that has created a plethora of recreational opportunities in rural communities, has affected the very social fabric of communities, forcing them to change the way they do business and to begin to understand the tourist.

Struggling Economy

The development of tourism is often seen as a panacea for the ills of a rural community. Rural communities have resorted to tourism in an attempt to fend off a variety of economic problems. It is interesting that although the overall economy of the United States is doing well, the rural economy has been struggling for many years. The rural economy is much different from the general economy, so much so, that it is not unusual for rural economies to struggle while the nation's general economy flourishes.

The problems, too numerous to list, that exist in rural areas include the flight of the young from the community, persistent poverty of residents and government, a lack of employment opportunities, and an overall lack of a stable infrastructure. As stated earlier, many rural communities have established tourism to generate much needed revenue, which, in turn, translates into jobs to keep people in the community.

Of course, it is not that simple. A community cannot simply decide to develop tourism, expecting that the next day all of its problems will be solved. Nor will tourism solve all of the rural problems in the country. However, as rural communities choose to develop tourism, rural leaders need to understand the tourism development process.

In order for rural leaders to understand tourism development, there must first exist examples of success, resource guides, and trained qualified people to teach tourism development. Unfortunately, there are too many rural communities attempting to develop tourism that do not have the necessary means to carry out the process.

The process of developing tourism in a rural community has not been clearly defined. Tourism research has emphasized marketing and the investigation of impacts. There is, however, very little knowledge of the process of developing tourism in the United States.

One prominent tourism researcher has pointed out that while we, as a profession, spend a lot of time researching the impacts and economics of tourism; we have largely ignored the development process. He goes on to suggest that it is difficult to understand tourism without first understanding the process that is involved in developing tourism.

Is it important to delineate the process of tourism development in a rural community? Will understanding the development process assist rural leaders in developing tourism, or give them the "right stuff" to develop tourism? It is difficult to answer these questions with any certainty, but understanding the process and the steps involved would surely help leaders — especially those in a rural community — to make informed decisions regarding tourism.

As communities develop tourism, the same mistakes are committed again and again; and most communities are forced to begin the process from square one. There is virtually no communication regarding the process, nor is there general information available that allows rural leaders to emulate what has been successful in other communities.

Because research has not concentrated on the process, there is not a great deal known. Many believe that a rural community makes the decision to develop tourism at a town meeting, a handful of the residents agree, and the next day the community begins the tourism development process. Needless to say, this is not exactly how the process works.

There is some research that has modeled the tourism development process. Perhaps the most well-known model is the one of tourism development proposed by Butler in 1980. He proposed that tourism was created and moved through a cycle, much like the lifecycle of a new product on the market.

Butler's model is often applied to tourism development, but there appears to be one shortcoming. His model does not take into account that the development of tourism in a rural community is much different from the development of tourism in an urban area. As stated earlier, rural communities, because of problems with the economy and the unique way that things are often done, are different. Thus, a generic model of tourism development may not necessarily apply to rural tourism development. As rural communities develop tourism, a process model that delineates the process exclusively for rural areas should be developed.

Process of Rural Tourism Development

Generally, from what little research is available, the process of rural tourism development usually begins when an individual or an organization believes that there is a resource in the community that would be of interest to tourists. That resource might be something natural, such as a park, or something constructed that might be unique to the area (for example, the covered bridges of Parke County, Indiana). This is considered the first stage of development.

The second stage involves "formalizing" the tourism process. Formal organizations would be started, local businesses would get involved, and the beginning of a plan to market tourism would start. During this stage, the individuals or groups involved often attempt to secure resources and look for funding to develop or enhance tourism attractions.

In the third stage, development has begun, and marketing is in full swing. Usually in a rural community, this is when you will see the development of special events and attractions. In addition, various tourism attractions will realize that instead of competing for the tourism dollar, they must work together to bring visitors to the community.

Finally, as tourism becomes a developed process, the community may establish a formal tourism organization, such as a convention and visitors bureau, which will usually implement tourism taxes. At this point, many communities have begun to work together to establish regional tourism, and tourism development becomes a centralized process in a rural community.

Tourism is usually developed in a rural community because of the influence of one person or a very small group of people. Contrary to certain research, it appears that rural tourism development is generally neither a community decision nor a decision that involves many people. It is a decision made by a person or persons who have the resources to provide for development.

For example, in several rural communities, it is a wealthy entrepreneur who makes the decision. In many communities, it is an area native who knows the community well and has an interest in it. Surprisingly, tourism development is not a community decision and may not be supported by all residents of the community.

While the concept of tourism development is changing everywhere, the changes felt in rural communities have been numerous. In the past, the government was responsible for community development, but today, because of myriad problems in a rural community, the government has its hands full.

The role of rural governments in the provision of infrastructure development is necessary, but tourism development often proceeds without the assistance of government. That is the new wave in rural development. And in rural tourism, a community must be able to develop tourism using resources from the government. Surprisingly, some research has shown that people who develop tourism don't desire this government involvement.

Of course, it is not possible to develop a standardized guide for the development of tourism in a rural community. When developing tourism, one cannot say that tourism development in a Nebraska community will mirror that of a community in Indiana. However, the different communities will develop tourism in similar ways, using similar methods.

Thus, what is needed is a resource guide that proposes different methods of tourism development and provides tried and true scenarios. Rural communities should be given the opportunity to obtain the resources that will assist them in developing tourism.

Tourism development tools include research, resource guides, how-to guides from successful communities, case studies, workshops, conferences, and training for rural leaders. The tourism development process must be delineated so that it can be illustrated and explained to rural community leaders. It is not possible to throw money at rural tourism and expect it to grow. Park, recreation, and tourism professionals must provide rural communities with the tools to develop tourism.

WHAT IS ERTD

ERTD is a collaborative partnership between 13 training institutions and public/private agencies drawn from 5 countries across Europe. The project is supported by the European Union through the Leonardo da Vinci programme, aimed at improving the vocational education systems of Europe.

Aim

The aim of the project is to develop and pilot new learning materials and a new course in rural tourism development which will be delivered on-line to course participants via a virtual campus. The programme will incorporate a variety of learning tasks, including the research, design and promotion of new rural tourism itineraries incorporating case studies to facilitate the learning process. The learning programmes will ensure skills and knowledge of participants meet the needs of the rural tourism sector and new opportunities for employment within it.

Target Group

The new learning programme developed within this pilot initiative is aimed at the following groups of participants

- Those owner/managers and employees involved in rural tourism activities, eg bed & breakfast, self catering holidays, agro-tourism
- Young people training in Leisure and Tourism
- Those people seeking to set up business within the rural tourism sector including the unemployed and those wishing to change direction

Primary Outcomes of the Project

- New learning programmes, course materials, to meet the needs of rural tourism enterprises which will be piloted, tested and evaluated across participating European countries
- The new courses will be developed using e-learning methodologies and will lead to a 'European' accreditation and certification offering participants recognition of the skills and competencies acquired. Certification will be secured in the following
- Management in Rural Tourism
- Development of Rural Tourist Attractions

12 GLOBALIZATION AND RURAL TOURISM

In globalization, all nations of the world share a global culture, a consequence of past choices. And, the economy has become increasingly global as well. Globalisation is the new buzzword that has come to dominate the world. The frontiers of the state with more dependent on the market economy and renewed faith in the private capital and resources, a process of structural adjustment spurred by the studies and influences of the World Bank and other International organisations have started in many of the developing countries.

However, within the global ecosystem are boundaries, which give form and structure to natural systems. Within the global culture are boundaries, which define different human values and perspectives of reality. And within the global economy are boundaries, which allow nations to reflect the differences in their natural ecosystems and social cultures in the structure and functioning of their economies.

Does globalization worsen income inequality or reduce it? In recent years, this simple yet stubborn question has spawned countless studies examining the link between economic openness and income gaps. However, these analyses typically use cross-country regressions and encounter two key problems. First, data on relevant indicators — such as national income-distribution measures — are often not compatible internationally because of differences in the definition of the variables and data collection methods.

Second, researchers often have a hard time accounting for variations in legal systems, political institutions, and culture that may affect economic growth and income inequality but may not be directly measurable. Indeed, some of these variables may interact with openness in affecting inequality and growth. As a result, evidence on the impact of globalization on inequality remains ambiguous.

Wei and Wu examine data for about 100 Chinese cities between 1988 and 1993, focusing on the gap between urban and rural incomes as a measure of income inequality. (They limit the study to cities that encompass urban areas plus adjacent rural counties.) Total income inequality in China can be decomposed into inequality between urban and rural areas, inequality within urban areas, and inequality within rural areas. A number of other studies have shown that the first component - the inequality between urban and rural incomes - explains 75-80 percent of the overall inequality in China in the last two decades.

It is sometimes asserted, based on China's aggregate statistics, that it is an example in which greater openness has led to an increase in inequality. Wei and Wu suggest that this is wrong because other factors, such as inflation, could account for the increase in inequality. A within-country study such as theirs can hold constant these nationwide factors. Wei and Wu find that "those cities that have had a greater increase in the trade-to-GDP ratio have also tended to witness a reduction, rather than an increase, in the urban-rural income inequality." In other words, openness to the global economy is associated with a reduction, not a worsening, of income disparities.

China is indeed a good case study: First, China offers "a quasi-natural experiment on the consequences of embracing globalization." Because of Deng Xiao-Ping's 1978 decision to open the Chinese economy to the rest of the world, the country's overall trade as a percentage of GDP skyrocketed from 8.5 percent in 1977 to 36.5 percent 22 years later. Second, China's size allows Wei and Wu to amass data from a large number of intra-national observations. This means that it would be more difficult to implement a similar study on economies such as Argentina, Bangladesh, or Costa Rica, three countries that also have increased their openness dramatically in the last two decades.

In addition to its economic lessons, China has geographic features that provide a methodological advantage. China is semi-landlocked with a coast on its Eastern and Southeastern sides. The differences across Chinese cities in terms of participation in international trade are, to a large extent, attributable to their varying distance from a major seaport. This is confirmed by the data.

Thus, the Chinese geography offers a plausible "instrumental variable" for local exposure to globalization. It would be more difficult to carry out a similar study on economies such as the United States or Indonesia whose access points to international trade are more diffused.

GLOBAL AGRICULTURAL ECONOMY

In a global agricultural economy, small farms will be replaced by large farms, which in turn will be controlled by giant multinational corporations. Small farmers quite simply will not be able to compete in a "free market" global economy. Many small farmers of the world rely on horticultural crops for their viability. Thus, the implications of globalization may be even more dramatic for horticulture than for most other agricultural sectors. But even more important, ecological and cultural boundaries are essential to the long run sustainability of agriculture. Thus, if all economic boundaries are removed, human life on earth, at least as we know it, will not be sustainable.

Globalisation has brought in new opportunities to developing countries. Greater access to developed country markets and technology transfer hold out promise improved productivity and higher living standard. But globalisation has also thrown up new challenges like growing inequality across and within nations, volatility in financial market and environmental deteriorations.

Another negative aspect of globalisation is that a great majority of developing countries remain removed from the process. Till the nineties the process of globalisation of the Indian economy was constrained by the barriers to trade and investment liberalisation of trade, investment and financial flows initiated in the nineties has progressively lowered the barriers to competition and hastened the pace of globalisation

Over the past decade, globalization has become a major public issue. Most of the recent controversy has centered on the World Trade Organization (WTO). The WTO was established in 1994, with authority to oversee international trade, administer free trade agreements, and settle trade disputes among member nations, replacing the General Agreement on Tariff and Trade (GATT).

However under the WTO, authority was greatly expanded to cover trade in services as well as merchandise – including protection of intellectual property rights. And, intellectual property rights have been interpreted to include the genetic code of living organisms. Also, the WTO has far greater authority over trade in agricultural commodities than had existed under the GATT. The implicit, if not explicit, objective in forming the WTO was to reduce and eventually remove all restraints to trade, in order to achieve a single "global free market."

"Globalization," as a concept, is far broader in meaning than is the concept of a "global free market." To "globalize," according to Webster's dictionary, means "to make worldwide in scope or application." The objective of the WTO is to create a single geographic market that is worldwide in scope, with a single set of trading rules that are worldwide in application. However, we cannot change the global economy without simultaneously affecting global ecology and global society. This is the crux of the current WTO controversy. What are the implications of a "global free market," not just for the world economy, but also for the world community and for the world itself?

We live in a global ecosystem, regardless of whether we like it or not. We have no choice; such is the nature of "nature." The atmosphere is global. Whatever we put in the air in one place eventually may find its way to any other place on the globe. Weather is global. The warming or cooling of the oceans in one part of the world affects the weather in another, which in turn affects the temperature of oceans elsewhere on the globe. All the elements of the biosphere are interrelated and interconnected, including its human elements. We are all members of the global community of nature. We have no choice in this matter.

Increasingly, we also live in a global "social" community. Global communications – print media, radio, television, and the Internet – have erased technical communications barriers among nations, resulting in the spread of common cultural values around the globe. Global travel has become faster, easier, and less expensive, resulting in greater person-to-person sharing of social and cultural values among nations. Consequently, the distinctiveness of national cultures has diminished. We seem to be moving toward universal membership in a common global culture.

However, in matters of society and culture we have the right and the responsibility to choose. We have the right to maintain whatever aspects of our unique local or national cultures and communities that we choose to keep. And we have the responsibility to protect this right against the economic or political forces pushing us toward a single global culture or social community.

We also seem to be moving toward a single global economy. International trade has increased dramatically over the past few decades, first under the various GATT agreements and now under the WTO. All of the national economies of the world are interconnected through their dependence upon each other for trade. Problems anywhere in the world economy, with Japan and Argentina being recent examples, create economic problems for nations all around the globe. However, the global economy is made up of numerous distinct markets – including national markets and various multinational trade groups, such as those defined by the North American Free Trade Agreement (NAFTA) and the European Union (EU). However, the implicit purpose of the WTO is to remove all restraints on trade among nations and among trade groups, and thus, to create a single global market.

In the matter of a single global market, we also have a right and a responsibility to choose. Every nation has the right to maintain those aspects of its local and national economies that it deems necessary to protect its resources and its people from exploitation. In a truly "global free market," the social and political boundaries that now protect nations from such economic exploitation would no longer exist. Again, to the crux of the WTO controversy, we must ask, "What are the implications of removing the economic boundaries among nations, thus creating a single global market?"

Perhaps, the best way to begin addressing this question is to examine the boundaries that currently restrain globalization and to ask why those boundaries are there in the first place. The boundaries that exist in nature, the ecological boundaries, were put there by natural processes. Such physical features as oceans, mountains, and even rivers and ridges, separate one physical bioregion from another.

Cultural and political boundaries are those things that define distinct "communities" of people – including cities, states, and nations. We established such boundaries to facilitate relationships among people within boundaries and to differentiate between relationships among people within a given "community" and their relationships with people in other "communities." Within cultural boundaries, relationships were nurtured to enhance social connectedness and personal security.

Boundaries "between" communities maintain some sense of identify, and thus, maintain diversity among different groups or collections of people. Diversity among communities maintains choices and opportunity for those of the current generation and for those of generations to follow. Historically, whenever one human culture or society has become dominate, but has then failed, alternative cultures and societies has always been available to restore health and growth, and thus, to provide resilience, and long run security for human progress. Without cultural diversity, there would have been nothing to replace the long line of failed societies of the past.

In earlier times, cultural and political boundaries tended to coincide with natural boundaries – oceans, mountains, rivers, and ridges. However during the industrial era, economic and political considerations have taken priority over natural boundaries in defining our social relationships. Wars have resulted in redrawing of national boundaries along lines that have little relationship to either topography or culture.

Towns and cities have expanded their boundaries with little regard for the best long run use of the land they have covered with highways, buildings, and parking lots. And with the trend toward a single "global community," the remaining social and cultural boundaries that still define different groups of people, with diverse social, ethical, and moral values, are being largely ignored.

With some notable exceptions, economic boundaries, over at least the past century, have been the same as national political boundaries. Historically, each nation has had its own currency, and has maintained economic relationships among those "within" nations as separate and distinct from economic relationships "among" nations. The British Empire of the early 1900s, which once included a fifth of the globe, might have been considered a single economic unit. More recently, the North American Free Trade Agreement and the European Union represent attempts to encompass several nations within a single economic boundary. But, most economic communities are still defined by the boundaries of single nations.

The basic purpose of economic boundaries is to promote "free trade" within the boundaries of communities and to carry out "selective trade" among those communities that are separated by economic boundaries. Economic diversity, as defined by economic boundaries, is necessary for division of labor and specialization.

If all national economies were to lose their distinctiveness, becoming as one, all potential gains from trade among nations would disappear. Historically, economic diversity among nations also has been considered a necessity to ensure choice and opportunity – to ensure health, growth, resilience, and long run security of the global economy. Humanity has not been willing to put all of its "economic eggs in one basket."

So, why have leaders of the major economic powers of the world decided now to put all their "economic eggs" in the "WTO basket?" The most logical answer seems to be that world leaders are now motivated more by short run economic consideration than by longer run concerns for human culture or for the natural environment.

In this respect, other nations quite likely are being misled by the "economic culture" of the U.S., which now dominates the global economy. The tremendous growth of the U.S. economy over the past century is widely attributed to our "competitive, free market" economy. Because of this growth, a new "culture of economics" now holds sway among many of the most economically powerful nations of the world.

Within this culture, economic boundaries are viewed as obstacles to trade, as limiting the ability of investors to maximize economic efficiency. "Free trade" among all nations would result in a more efficient global economy, they say, thus benefiting all people of the world. Current barriers to trade, they say, usually are nothing more than artificial, political restraints designed to protect specific individuals and industries within nations from economic competition with more efficient producers in other nations. Thus, the WTO should work to remove such barriers, allowing the most efficient producers in the world to produce the world's goods and services, resulting in the lowest possible cost of goods and services to consumers everywhere – so they claim.

Such claims are based on economic theories of trade that historically have made "free trade" something of a "sacred tenet" of economics. This is true particularly among the more conservative of economists, whose views are now in vogue. Contemporary "free trade theory" has its foundation in the early 1800s, primarily in the writing of British economist, David Ricardo.

Ricardo showed that when two individuals choose to trade, each is better off after the trade than before. People have different tastes and preferences, and thus, each person values the same things somewhat differently. So, if I value something you now own more highly than I value something I own, and you value the thing that I own more highly than you value the thing you own, we will both gain by trading. I will get something that I value more than the thing I now own and so will you.

The same concept can be used to show the potential gains from trade associated with economic specialization. For example, one farmer may be a more efficient producer of one crop, e.g. tomatoes, and another farmer may be a more efficient producer of another, e.g. green peas. If so, one farmer can then specialize in green peas and the other in tomatoes. The better tomato producer can then trade tomatoes for peas and the green pea producer can trade peas for tomatoes, and they both will be better off than if they each tried to produce both peas and tomatoes.

Even if one farmer is a better producer of both peas and tomatoes, the other farmer will have a "comparative advantage" in producing one or the other. Let's say the first farmer could produce either 4 tons of green peas or 80 tons of tomatoes on a hectare of land and a given amount of labor, and capital. Assume a second farmer could only produce 3.3 tons of green peas or 60 tons of tomatoes on a hectare of land using the same amount of labor and capital – not as much of either as the first farmer.

Although the arithmetic gets messy, if the second farmer specializes in peas and the first in tomatoes, and they trade their surpluses to each other, both will be better off than if each produces some peas and some tomatoes. Of course the real world is much more complex than this simple "two producer, two commodity" example, but this simple one-on-one trade situation is still at the heart of contemporary economic trade theory.

So, if both traders gain from specialization and trade, what's wrong with "free trade?" The problems arise because "free trade" between two independent individuals, in the context of the early

1800s, does not accurately reflect the reality of trade among nations in the early 2000s.

First, trade is truly free only if both partners are "free not to trade." Participants in "free trade" must have an "interdependent" relationship. Interdependence implies that people relate to each other "by choice," not "by necessity." If one trading partner is dependent on another, the dependent partner may have no choice but to do whatever is necessary to maintain the relationship. "Interdependent" relationships can only be formed between two otherwise independent entities. When both are independent, neither is compelled to either form or maintain the relationship. Under such circumstances, trading relationships are formed only if they are beneficial to both and continue only so long as they remain beneficial to both.

Trading under conditions of coercion, under explicit or implied threats of retribution, is not free trade. The school kid that "trades lunches" with the bully, under threat of bodily harm, is not participating in free trade. Neither is a weak nation that trades with a strong nation, under the threat of denial of military protection from some global tyrant. Nor is it "free trade" if one nation is dependent on the other for its economic wellbeing, as in cases where one nation has built up large debts to another.

Poor nations are made dependent on rich nations by their lack of economic wealth, economic infrastructure, and technological advantage, regardless of their inherent worth to humanity. In many cases, rich nations are able to exploit the workers and resources of poor nations through trade, because the poor see no other way to avoid physical depravation or starvation of their people. Trade when one party feels compelled to trade is not "free trade." Coerced trade is not "free trade."

Second, "free trade" assumes "informed trade." Both parties must understand the ultimate consequences of their actions. If a car dealer trades cars with a customer, knowing his car is a gas-guzzler, needs lots of repairs, and is unsafe to drive, and trades the car without informing the customer, this is not a "free trade." When a developed nation encourages a lesser-developed nation to produce for export markets, knowing that such production will lead to exploitation of their natural and human resources, and does not inform them of the consequences, this is not free trade.

The "leaders" of the lesser-developed nations may reap benefits from such trades, often including bribes or payoffs from the outside exploiters, but the resources of the lesser-developed nation will be exploited rather than developed. The people will be left with fewer opportunities for developing their country than they had before. The exploiters know the consequences but the exploited do not. Uninformed trade is not "free trade."

Third, "free trade," in economic theory, implies that the decision is made by an individual, not a collection of people or a nation. Individuals are whole people, presumably absent of unresolved internal conflicts regarding the relative values of items to be traded. A person trades only if they decide trading is good for them as a whole. Nations cannot think with one mind or speak with one voice.

Nations, as large collections of individuals, may make and carry out trade agreements to which a substantial portion of the nation's population is opposed, both before and after trade takes place. The economic rational for such agreements is that if the economic benefits to those who favor trade more than offset the economic costs to those who oppose it, the nation as a whole will benefit from the trade.

Economics is incapable of dealing with social consequences of trade, such as equity or justice. In economics, a nation is said to gain from trade if those who benefit from trade "could" compensate those who lose and still have something left over. Of course, the gainers are under no legal obligation to compensate the losers, and rarely, if ever, do so.

And in economics, it doesn't matter that the rich are made richer and the poor are made poorer. In economics, it doesn't really matter how many people are made "relatively" worse or better off by trade, as long as trade results in greater total wealth and growth of the overall economy. Free trade doesn't address issues of social equity or justice.

Finally, the foundational principles of economic trade theory are rooted in a "barter economy" – people "trade" things rather than buy or sell things. In an international currency economy, comparative advantages in trade can be distorted by fluctuations in currency exchange rates that have nothing to do with relative productivity.

Such fluctuations can cause the exports from one nation to become more or less costly to importers from another nation for reasons totally unrelated to changes in production efficiency. Under such conditions, "free markets" do not result in efficient resource use. Trade theory assumes differences in monetary prices reflect differences in real value.

In classic trade theory, also, each trading partner uses their individual resources, land, labor, capital, technology, etc. to do whatever they do best – to realize their comparative advantage. No consideration is given to the possibility that one nation might instead transfer some of their resources, such as capital and production technology, to another nation where they might generate even greater profits. Mobility of capital and technology, hallmarks of today's global economy, eliminates the "comparative advantage" of higher cost nations, forcing them to import from lower cost nations, devaluing both land and labor in the higher cost nation to globally competitive levels. The classical economic concepts of comparative advantage did not anticipate international mobility of capital and technology.

Because of all these inconsistencies between economic theory and economic reality, the theory of economic "free trade" does not reflect the reality of "international free trade" today. Perhaps more important, opposition and open defiance of the WTO, from countries around the globe, indicates that any further expansion of trade, being forced upon unwilling people by the WTO, almost certainly will "not" be "free trade," but "coerced trade."

So what are the implications of market globalization for international agriculture, and specifically, for the sustainability of small horticultural farms? First, the implications will be different in different parts of the world, because of the wide diversity in current size and ownership structure of horticultural production units in different countries. Obviously, large differences exist between agriculture in the "developed" and "developing" countries of the world. However, significant differences also exist within these two communities of nations.

The European Union (EU) and the United States provide a convenient example of contrasts within developed economies. Horticultural production in Eastern Europe is carried out in predominantly family-based enterprises. Historically, fruit and vegetable farms were small, family operations, located close to the cities, and focused on producing for local consumption. Over time, however, some of the more specialized operations expanded in size, as lower transportation costs allowed them to compete in more-distant markets. In Europe today, small-scale family operations still co-exist with these larger specialized operations, with each focusing on different markets.

Approximately 1.8 million farms in the EU produced fruit and vegetables in the early 1990s. Many of these obviously were small family enterprises oriented toward home consumption, as they averaged only 1.3 ha. in size overall. Some 100,000 of these were classified as commercial operations specializing in production of vegetables, averaging 4.2 ha. in size, and 350,000 were commercial operations specializing in production of fruit, averaging 7.9 ha. in size.

Horticulture in the United States has experienced the same basic trends as in the EU – toward geographic specialization and large-scale production. However, operations in the US tend to be larger than in Europe. The US 1992 Census of Agriculture reported 29,605 farms producing vegetable and melons, 99,514 farms producing fruit and nuts, and 39,712 producing various other horticultural crops. The average size of US horticultural farms was

21 ha. for fruit and nut farms and 50 ha. for vegetable and melon farms – far larger than in the EU.

Comparable data are not available for many of the developing countries. However over the past decade, the fastest growing fruit and vegetable regions of the world have been Asia (particularly China) and South America (particularly, Brazil and Chile). Asia now accounts for more than 60 percent of worldwide vegetable output, and China alone accounts for about 25 percent of world production of apples. With the exception of a few large corporate operations that serve export markets, available data indicate the vast majority of production units in Asia and South America are smaller, family operations serving local markets.

In general, regardless of the region of the world or the segment of agriculture considered, the vast majority of all farms are still small farms, with many still serving local markets. However, the vast majority of total agricultural output is accounted for by a small proportion of larger, specialized commercial operations, oriented toward serving global markets. And increasingly, these large, export-oriented agricultural operations are controlled, if not owned outright, by giant multinational corporations.

As diversified family farmers have been replaced by large, specialized production units, independent food processors and wholesalers have been displaced by giant food processing and distribution firms. These large food processing and distribution operations more recently have combined, through various types of alliances and joint ventures, into five or six even-larger "global food chain clusters." As the four or five dominate global food retailers link up with existing "global food chain clusters," they increasingly will control all phases of the global food system from "conception to consumption," including agricultural production.

The two dominant trends in agriculture today, globalization and corporate consolidation, are not just coincidental, but almost certainly are intentional. Trade negotiators for the more industrialized nations, the US in particular, are the driving force within the WTO demanding ultimate removal of all social and ecological barriers to trade. The support of multinational agribusiness corporations is the primary motivating force behind these negotiators. With all political constraints to trade removed, the multinational corporations would be free to treat the world as a single production area and single market, and thus to maximize profits globally.

The world economy envisioned under the WTO presumably would operate much as a national economy. "International commerce" would resemble "interstate commerce," and no individual member nation would be allowed to have laws interfering with such commerce. Under the WTO, nothing could be arbitrarily excluded from "international commerce." The WTO would decide what nations can and cannot exclude from the world marketplace. And, no seller or buyer would be allowed to offer different prices or conditions of trade to different nations, for any reasons.

Under such rules of trade, a nation could not subsidize its agriculture by any means that might be trade distorting; that is, it couldn't subsidize producers of one commodity more than it subsidizes producers of another. A nation could not establish environmental, health, or safety standards for its production processes that were more restrictive than those specified by the WTO.

A nation could not close its borders to WTO approved "cultural exports" from other nations – movies, television programs, clothes, and magazines – no matter how repulsive they may be to some residents of that nation. A nation could not refuse to allow its natural resources, such as minerals, oil, or even water, to be sold to another nation. And, the WTO would stand ready to enforce merchandise patents and intellectual property rights globally, regardless of whether the people of the world agree that all things, such as genetic life forms, should be patented. These are but some of the many potential consequences of the WTO vision of a single global economy.

In essence, removal of national economic boundaries would open the world to "corporate colonization." Historically, a "colony" has been defined as a geographic territory, acquired by conquest or settlement by a people or government previously alien to that territory (Encarta, 1998).

In general, a colonial relationship is created when one entity extends its sovereignty and imposes control over another people or territory. In the case of "corporate colonization," it is the *corporation*, rather than a *people* or *government* that extends its sovereignty and imposes its control over the *economies* of nations. Nations lose control over their individual economies as their economic boundaries are removed, allowing the multinational corporations, previously alien to their countries, to expand across political boundaries at will.

The potential for economic colonization is inherent, so long as the world is composed of nations at radically different stages of economic and technological development. Those in the more developed economies will always be tempted to dominate those in the less developed economies. The emergence of multinational corporations, lacking a strong affiliation to any nation, makes those in the less developed areas or all nations vulnerable to global corporate domination. Such disparities in power, however, only make colonization possible – not necessary or inevitable. The powerful are not always able to expand and dominate the weak, as long as the weak have the political means to resist. Once the economic boundaries are removed, however, there will be no political means to resist.

As with political colonialism, there are strong arguments both for and against economic colonialism. Clearly, multinational corporations can bring numerous economic benefits to people in less developed economies, including greater access to investment capital, more employment opportunities, and higher personal incomes. A stronger economy also provides opportunities for governments to spend more for public transportation, health care, education, national defense, police protection, and other social welfare programs.

However, reliance on outside corporate investors for capital and technologies brings with it significant social and ecological risks. As with political colonization, life-styles are disrupted, cultures are destroyed, and entire communities, nations, and races of people may be economically subjugated by the corporations. A nation's natural resources – minerals, petroleum, forests, biological diversity, soils – may be exploited to maximize corporate profits, because there is no long term corporate commitment to any particular people, place, or culture.

Decades after political colonization has ended, many so-called Third World countries still harbor a deep resentment, sometimes hatred, toward their former "colonial masters," in spite of the numerous economic, health, technological, and educational benefits they received. There certainly is no reason to believe that an after-the-fact assessment of benefits and costs will be any less condemning of the corporate colonization process.

Under contemporary international standards of human rights, political colonialism is no longer considered excusable – no matter what the potential economic or social benefits. Colonialism conflicts directly with inherent rights of national sovereignty and self-determination. The 19th-century empire builders, however, believed they had a moral responsibility to rule the "backward peoples" of the world, in order to bring them the fruits of Western civilization.

Many in the more developed nations today believe they have a moral responsibility to develop the "less developed economies" of the world, in order to bring them Western prosperity. The industrial nations have tried, without much success, to impose their industrial economic model on the rest of the world through various government- and foundation-funded international economic development programs.

From an international policy perspective, economic colonization by multinational corporations is but another means of developing the "less-developed economies" of the world. The next stage of development, for most less-developed countries, is the transition out of agriculture and into manufacturing.

This transition cannot take place until agriculture is industrialized, making it possible for the agricultural sector to produce more food with fewer farmers, thus freeing farmers to work in the factories and offices of the new industrial economies. Agricultural globalization will make it possible for the agribusiness corporations to industrialize the agriculture of these lesser-developed economies. Thus, agricultural globalization is seen as a necessary prerequisite to global economic development.

Before addressing the implications of agricultural globalization on sustainable horticultural farms, we must address the sustainability of agriculture in general. First, any form of sustainable development, including sustainable agriculture, must meet the needs of the present while leaving equal or better opportunities for the future. To meet this standard of sustainability, a system of production and distribution must be ecologically sound, economically viable, and socially responsible. Lacking any one of these three aspects, a system quite simply is not sustainable over the long run. Globalization is a strategy designed for short-run economic exploitation, not for long run societal sustainability.

A sustainable food system, to be ecologically sound, must work in harmony with nature – not attempt to dominate or conquer nature. Nature is inherently diverse. Diversity in nature is necessary to support life within nature. "Boundaries" in nature define the diversity of landscapes, life forms, and resources needed to support healthy, natural, sustainable production processes. Fence rows, streams, and ridges define unique agro-ecosystems within which nature can sustain different types of human enterprises.

Economic globalization ultimately will result in removal of fence rows, diversion of streams, and leveling of ridges, to facilitate standardization of functions and homogenization of production processes. The natural boundaries needed for sustainability will be removed to achieve greater economic efficiency. Economic globalization ultimately will destroy ecological sustainability.

A sustainable food system, in being socially responsible, must function in harmony with human "communities," including towns, cities, and nations. Humanity is inherently diverse. Diversity among people is necessary for "interdependent" relationships – relationships of choice among unique, independent individuals. Although we have our humanity in common, each person is unique, and we need unique human "communities" within which to express our uniqueness.

Social and cultural boundaries define those "communities" – towns, states, and nations. Globalization will remove those boundaries and will homogenize global culture and society. The natural boundaries needed to sustain social responsibility will be removed to achieve greater economic efficiency. Economic globalization ultimately will destroy social sustainability.

A sustainable food system, to be economically viable, must facilitate harmonious relationships among people and between people and their natural environment. The inherent diversity of nature and of humanity must be reflected in diversity of the economy. Although potential gains from specialization are real, such gains are based on the premise that people and resources are inherently diverse, with unique abilities to contribute to the economy.

Competitive capitalism is based on the premise that individual entrepreneurs make individual decisions and accept individual responsibility for their actions. If globalization is allowed to destroy the boundaries that define the diversity of nature and people, then it will destroy both the efficiency and sustainability of the economy. Economic globalization ultimately will destroy even economic sustainability.

In a global agricultural economy, large farms will continue to displace smaller farm in the global marketplace. Increasingly, the larger farms will be controlled by giant multinational corporations. Many small farms depend on sales of internationally traded commodities to provide cash farm income, in developed as well as less-developed countries.

The most important aspect of their farming operation may be its non-cash contributions to their quality of life. In less-developed countries, the major non-cash contribution of farms may be food, clothing, and shelter, while in other countries it may be a healthy environment, privacy and security, and an independent life-style. In both cases, however, the economic viability of the farm may depend on cash income from sales of internationally trade commodities.

Under globalization and corporate colonialism, small independent family farms quite simply will not have access to markets for internationally traded commodities. Essentially all such commodities will be produced under comprehensive contracts offered by corporations linked to one of the "global food clusters." Only the larger farming operations will be able to secure such contracts, and in many countries, such operations may be corporately owned and operated.

Commercial horticultural markets will become geographically specialized globally. In those areas of the world with an economic comparative advantage in horticulture, the larger farming operations will be consolidated and absorbed into one of the "global food clusters" – through contract or outright ownership. In those areas lacking a comparative advantage in horticulture, the commercial market infrastructure for horticultural crops will be dismantled due to lack of use.

Thus, small family horticultural operations will be denied access to markets for internationally traded commodities in both cases. Small farmers worldwide rely on horticultural crops not only for their in-home own use but also for cash income, and thus, for their economic viability. Thus, globalization has important implications not only for the economic viability of small-scale horticulture but for the sustainability of small family farms everywhere.

The implications of market globalization and corporate colonialism are no more acceptable than were the implications of earlier attempts at cultural globalization and political colonialism. But with such powerful economic and political forces promoting globalization, how can we ordinary people expect to stop it. First, we can help people realize that the undeniable existence of a global ecosystem, a global society, and a global economy does not justify market globalization – i.e., the removal of all economic boundaries among nations. Natural boundaries are necessary to ensure ecological integrity. Cultural boundaries are necessary to ensure social responsibility. And economic boundaries are necessary to ensure long run economic viability. Without boundaries, the world will tend toward entropy – toward a world without form, without structure, without order, and without life.

Every nation has both a right and a responsibility to protect its people and its resources from exploitation, just as every person has a right and responsibility to protect their person and property from exploitation. Globalization would deny these most fundamental of human rights to the "communities" of people that constitute the nations of the world. People need to have healthy relationships with each other and with the earth, but healthy relationships are relationships of choice, not relationships of coercion. Global society needs a world forum, such as the WTO might be – not to remove boundaries, but to ensure that every person of every nation is protected from economic exploitation. We must reclaim our rights to individual and national sovereignty.

Other things we can do to fight globalization are more tangible and practical – and many of these things are particularly relevant to horticultural producers and marketers. We can all help develop more sustainable, local alternatives, which will reduce our reliance on multinational corporations. For example, millions of farmers and consumers all around the world are already joining forces to develop more sustainable, local food systems.

These people come together regularly within their local communities at farmers markets, CSAs, community gardens, and at other venues where farmers and consumers meet around food. The central focus of many, if not most, of these alternative food systems is horticultural crops – vegetables, fruits, flowers, etc. The sustainability of small family horticultural farms in the future will depend on the evolution of these alternative niche markets of today. As these markets evolve, small horticultural farms of the future may well become still greater in number, far more important to human nutrition and health, and even more profitable for small farmers.

Perhaps one of the most common of misperceptions today is that niche markets make up only a small part of total markets and that niche marketing will always be marginal to the marketing mainstream. In reality, all consumer markets are niche markets, because all individual consumers have different tastes and preferences. It's a fundamental principle of economics, the utility or economic value of anything depends of individuality – on "who" has it and "who" wants it, and not just on what it is, where it is, and when it's available.

The industrial food system has focused on minimizing the cost of changing form, place, and time – on efficiency of processing, transportation, packaging, and storage – through systems mass production and distribution. In attempting to minimize costs, food production and distribution systems have become highly specialized, standardized, and centralized, and people have been treated as if we all had much the same tastes and preferences. Industrial systems are inherently inefficient in doing a lot of different things for a lot of different individuals.

As we move into the post-industrial era of economic development, however, the focus is shifting from minimizing costs to maximizing individual consumer satisfaction. Industrial foods have emphasized superficial product differentiation and "mass-produced convenience" – packaging, preparation, and home delivery – to make industrial foods more acceptable to individual consumers. Ultimately, however, the bulk of the food market will go to those who give individual consumers the foods that they actually want – choices of food with flavor, freshness, nutrition, and integrity – not just food that is quick, convenient, and cheap. Small family horticultural farms that are focused on niche markets are on the frontier of the new post-industrial food system.

Thus, successful small farmers of the future must give an even higher priority to local markets in developing more sustainable farming systems. They must realize they simply will not be able to sustain their farming operation by competing with the multinational food corporations in the emerging global economy. They must focus on those quality attributes of products that the multinational corporations cannot match with the industrial system of production and distribution – such as nutrition, freshness, flavor, and food safety.

13 Rural Wine and Food Tourism

Sonoma County wine is wine made in Sonoma County, California, USA. County names in the United States automatically qualify as legal appellations of origin for wine produced from grapes grown in that county and do not require registration with the United States Department of the Treasury, Alcohol and Tobacco Tax and Trade Bureau.

Grapes were planted in Sonoma County at Fort Ross as early as 1812. Padre Jose Altimira planted several thousand grape vines at Mission San Francisco Solano in what is now the city of Sonoma, in southern Sonoma County. Cuttings from the Sonoma mission vineyards were carried throughout the northern California area to start new vineyards.

By the time of the Bear Flag Revolt in Sonoma and the subsequent annexation of California by the United States in 1854, wine grapes were an established part of agriculture in the region. The vineyards of General Mariano Vallejo, military Governor of Mexican California and based in Sonoma, were producing an annual income of $20,000 at that time. The grape varietals planted would not be considered premium varietals today.

In 1855, a Hungarian named Agoston Haraszthy arrived and purchased the Salvador Vallejo vineyard in Sonoma Valley, renaming it Buena Vista. Commissioned in 1861 by the California legislature to study viticulture in Europe, he returned with more than 100,000 cuttings of premium grape varietals. Many of the immigrants to the area were Northern Italian or from other wine-growing regions of Europe. After the Civil War and before Prohibition, wineries such as Bundschu, Foppiano, Korbel, Simi, Gundlach, Quitzow and Sebastiani were established that still exist.

In the 1920s there were 256 wineries in Sonoma County, with more than 22,000 acres (89 km^2) in production. During the Prohibition period, however, commercial winemaking declined. At the repeal of Prohibition in 1933, fewer than 50 wineries in Sonoma County survived. Even as late as the 1960s, only 12,000 acres (49 km^2) were vineyards. But wine consumption in American began to grow, and by 1999 Sonoma County had over 49,000 acres (198 km^2) of vineyards owned by more than 750 growers and 180 bonded wineries. Of the 250 wineries existing in 2007, over half are less than 20 years old.

WINEMAKING

In 2004, growers harvested 165,783 tons (150,396 tonnes) of wine grapes worth US$310 million. In 2006 the Sonoma County grape harvest amounted to 216,000 tons, worth US$430 million. About 73% of Sonoma County's agricultural production is growing wine grapes—60,302 acres (244 km^2) of vineyards, with over 1100 growers. The most common varieties planted are Chardonnay, Cabernet Sauvignon, and Pinot Noir, though the area is also known for its Merlot and Zinfandel.

Vineyard

A vineyard is a plantation of grape-bearing vines, grown mainly for winemaking, but also raisins, table grapes and non-alcoholic grape juice. The science, practice and study of vineyard production is known as viticulture.

A vineyard is often characterised by its terroir, a French term loosely translating as "a sense of place" that refers to the specific geographical and geological characteristics of grapevine plantations, which may be imparted in the wine.

The quest for vineyard efficiency has produced a bewildering range of systems and techniques in recent years. Due to the often much more fertile New World growing conditions, attention has focussed heavily on managing the vine's more vigorous growth. Innovation in *palissage* (training of the vine, usually along a trellis, and often referred to as "canopy management") and pruning and thinning methods (which aim to optimize the Leaf Area/Fruit (LA/F) ratio relative to a vineyard's microclimate) have largely replaced more general, traditional concepts like "yield per unit area" in favor of "maximizing yield of desired quality". Many of these new techniques have since been adopted in place of traditional practice in the more progressive of the so-called "Old World" vineyards.

Other recent practices include spraying water on vines to protect them from sub-zero temperatures (aspersion), new grafting techniques, soil slotting, and mechanical harvesting. Such techniques have made possible the development of wine industries in New World countries such as Canada. Today there is increasing interest in developing organic, ecologically sensitive and sustainable vineyards. Biodynamics has become increasingly popular in viticulture. The use of drip irrigation in recent years has expanded vineyards into areas which were previously unplantable. As a consequence of irrigation, yields are more consistent and vintage years virtually irrelevant.

For well over half a century Cornell University, the University of California, Davis, and California State University, Fresno, among others, have been conducting scientific experiments to improve viticulture and educating practitioners. The research includes developing improved grape varieties and investigating pest control. The International Grape Genome Program is a multi-national effort to discover a genetic means to improving quality, increasing yield and providing a "natural" resistance to pests.

The implementation of mechanical harvesting is often stimulated by changes in labor laws, labor shortages, and bureaucratic complications. It can be expensive to hire labor for short periods of time, which does not square well with the need to reduce production costs and harvest quickly, often at night. However, very small vineyards, incompatible widths between rows of grape vines and steep terrain hinder the employment of machine harvesting even more than the resistance of traditional views which reject such harvesting.

There are also changes in the kinds of grapes grown. For example, in Chile, large areas of low-quality grapes have been replaced with such grapes as Chardonnay and Cabernet Sauvignon. Grape changes are often in response to changing consumer demand but sometimes result from vine pull schemes designed to promote vineyard change. Alternatively, the development of "T" budding now permits the grafting of a different grape variety onto existing rootstock in the vineyard, making it possible to switch varieties within a two year period.

Local legislation often dictates which varieties are selected, how they are grown, whether vineyards can be irrigated and exactly when grapes can be harvested, all of which in serves to reinforce tradition. Of course, changes in the law can change which grapes are planted. For example, during Prohibition in the U.S. (1920–1933), vineyards in California expanded sevenfold to meet the increasing demand for home-brewing. However, they were largely planted in varieties with tough skins that could be transported across the country to home wine-makers and the resulting wine was of low quality.

Terroir refers to the combination of natural factors associated with any particular vineyard. These factors include such things as soil, underlying rock, altitude, slope of hill or terrain, orientation toward the sun, and microclimate (typical rain, winds, humidity, temperature variations, etc.) No two vineyards have exactly the same terroir, although any difference in the resulting wine may be virtually undetectable.

Vineyards are often on hillsides and on soil of marginal value to other plants. A common saying is that "the worse the soil, the better the wine." Planting on hillsides, especially those facing south, is most often in an attempt to maximize the amount of sunlight that falls on the vineyard. For this reason some of the best wines come from vineyards planted on quite steep hills, conditions which would make most other agricultural products uneconomic. The stereotypical vineyard site for wine grapes (in the Northern hemisphere) is a hillside in a dry climate with a southern exposure, good drainage to reduce unnecessary water uptake, and balanced pruning to force the vine to put more of its energy into the fruit, rather than foliage.

What is Vignette?

A vignette is a 500 square metre vineyard which is part of a larger consolidated vineyard. Investors purchase a piece of land within a vineyard, and outsource the grape maintenance and production operations to an outside grape grower or wine producers. Because they are contracting under a cooperative structure, they benefit from economies of scale and hence cheaper labour and operational costs.

FOOD TOURISM

Food tourism is something that is becoming more commonly understood. But how would someone decide where to go, and what to see? It's fairly simple, actually. Tourists should first decide which type of cuisine they would like to try. Start by figuring out which food they love the best and by doing a little research. Then, after the tourist arrives in the city, they should seek the advice of others. Ask the local cab driver or the hotel clerk where the best places are to eat. Don't think that you have to stick to gourmet restaurants. Sometimes the smaller restaurants that are on the side streets are the best places to try traditional cuisine.

Egypt is a large country in Africa that is connected to Asia by the Sinai Peninsula. It has long been known for being the home of Egyptian civilization, with mysterious pyramids, spooky mummies and interesting hieroglyphs. Cairo is the destination of most tourists, as it is the home of not only the Egyptian Museum, but the Giza Pyramids as well. Luxor is where the gateway to the Valley of the

Kings lies, and Siwa is a hidden oasis town that has much to offer it's visitors. Egypt is truly a country that caters to adventurers and casual travelers alike.

Traditional Cuisine

Like much of the eastern Mediterranean countries, traditional Egyptian cuisine consists of many different herbs and spices. Lamb is the popular protein and vegetables are often stuffed and eaten as a side dish.

Traditional Dishes

One dish that is considered to be the national dish of Egypt is called ful medames. Ful medames is a dish that is usually eaten for the breakfast meal. Fava beans are cooked in a copper pot extremely slowly and for a long period of time. This makes the beans easy to mash. After they have been mashed, olive oil and garlic is added. Onion, garlic and lemon juice are also used to season the mashed fava beans. Baladi bread is sometimes served alongside the dish, as well as hard boiled eggs and other vegetables.

Shawerma is another popular Egyptian dish. It is a sandwich that is made up using either lamb, chicken or goat. A large piece of meat is skewed with onion and tomato on top. It is roasted for a number of hours. The meat is then shaved off in thin slices and is put into a pita bread or other flatbread.

Sometimes hummus, Amba sauce or pickled vegetables are put into the bread. It is often eaten as fast food and is available on a number of carts around the larger cities. Dukkah is another quick snack. It is a mixture that is created using nuts, seeds and other spices. Often pita bread is dipped into olive oil and then the mixture. This gives the bread a different taste and is extremely nutritious to eat.

Kushari is a popular dish and is served in most of the restaurants in the country. Kushari is created using a base of lentils, chickpeas, macaroni and rice. These are topped with garlic and tomato sauce and fried onions are often put on top. It is similar to the Western spaghetti and meatballs meal, but has a much more spicy taste.

FOOD IN DENMARK

Denmark is a small country located in Northern Europe. It used to be the home of the Vikings, which meant that it was a major power in Europe. Now, however, Denmark is a modern nation that is helping with the economic integration of Europe. Most tourists head to Copenhagen, which is one of the major cities of the country. Others head to Legoland, which is perfect for families or Lego-lovers to visit, and Ribe, the oldest town in Denmark.

Traditional Cuisine

Traditional Denmark cuisine is much like the cuisine of Norway and Germany. Most dishes are very heavy and have a lot of meat and carbohydrates in them. People survived on the foods that they could grow until the 1860's, when Denmark finally became a member of trade with other nations. This means that vegetables and fruits played a large part in the majority of early dishes.

Traditional Dishes

The first meal of the day is usually buttered bread that is served with cheese, jam and coffee. Sometimes salami is served as well. Some Danish people eat cereal with a crumbled bread on top, or an porridge. On a special occasion, morgenbord is served. This is a buffet of different foods that are laid out during an anniversary or birthday. It will have a number of different breakfast selections on it.

Smorrebrod is a type of sandwich that is eaten during the lunch hour. It is a buttered rye bread that is topped with cold cuts, meat or cheese. There are a number of different combinations that can be made, but all of these open sandwiches are created using a base of a dark buttered bread and a meat or cheese. Just like the Danish have a special celebratory meal for breakfast, so do they for lunch.

Kolde bord, or cold table, is a smorgasbord of lunch items that are served on a large table. Different items, such as pickled herring, Danish sausage, Veal medallion, cold cuts, and different breads, are laid out for people to choose from.

Dinner is the main meal of the day, and is when the family gathers together. Regular dinners may include dishes such as frikadeller. Frikadeller are a Danish meatball that is made using ground veal or pork, onions, eggs, and spices. It is made into balls, flattened, and fried in pork fat. They are often served with potatoes and gravy or red cabbage. These are also a popular dish in a smorgasbord.

Christmas Lunch

Christmas time is a special time in a Danish household. A Christmas lunch is often served. This lunch can be for family members or for a business. It includes traditional smorgasbord items, such as liver, cold cuts, salads, cheeses, and fruit. One thing that separates a Julefrokost from a traditional lunch buffet is the selskabssang, or party song. These are songs that are sung during the meal, making the occasion extremely festive.

FOOD COURT

A food court is a (usually) indoor plaza or common area within a facility that is contiguous with the counters of multiple food vendors and provides a common area for self-serve dining. Food courts may be found in shopping malls and airports, and in various regions (such as Asia and Africa) may be a standalone development. In some places of learning such as high schools and universities, food courts have also come to replace or complement traditional cafeterias. The average cost of a meal per person in an American food court in 2004 was $6.

Food courts consist of a number of vendors at food stalls or service counters. Meals are ordered at one of the vendors and then carried to a common dining area. Food is usually eaten with plastic silverware, and sporks are sometimes utilized to avoid the necessity of providing both forks and spoons. Typical North American and European food courts have mostly fast food chains such as McDonald's and Sbarro, with perhaps a few smaller private vendors. Cuisines and choices are varied, with larger food courts offering more global choices. Asian and African food courts are mostly private vendors that offer local cuisine. In Singapore, food courts and hawker centers are the people's main eating choice when dining out. Many food courts have several shops which sell prepared meals for shoppers to take home and reheat, making the food court a daily stop for some shoppers.

Common materials used in constructing food courts are tile, linoleum, Formica, stainless steel, and glass, all of which facilitate easy cleanup. The second-floor food court at the Paramus Park shopping mall in New Jersey, which opened in March 1974, has been credited as the first successful shopping mall food court. Built by The Rouse Company, one of the leading mall building companies of the time, it followed an unsuccessful attempt at the Plymouth Meeting Mall in 1971, which reportedly failed because it was "deemed too small and insufficiently varied."

14 Regional Cooperation in Rural Tourism

Sustainable tourism should be a part of the economy in rural areas that runs all other economic activities. Tourism which is not sustainable will devastate nature and the result will be a loss of tourists' interest in such destinations. In contrast, in a favorable ecological environment tourists will feel comfortable and together with local residents will actively participate in the development of touristic culture and protection from environmental devastation.

Asia's tourism industry professionals intend setting up a platform to boost regional cooperation and achieve common economic growth and a prosperous tourism sector across the vast continent. The five hundred honourable participants from more than thirty countries and regions who gathered in the prestigious scenic city of Guilin in south China's Guangxi Zhuang Autonomous Region, at the Bo'ao Forum for Asia - Tourism Conference discussed prospects and policies for Asian tourism and adopted the Guilin Declaration.

Asia is the largest continent in the world, where 60 percent of the world's population is concentrated. It boasts the age-old history and culture, breathtaking natural landscapes, and vivid, diversified and fascinating ethnic features.

Tourism has become an integral component part of all economies in the region, drawing more and more worldwide attention. Meanwhile, the tourist industry in the region is also confronted with a number of stark challenges including security and the need for sustainable tourism. Forum participants believe that more concrete and diversified regional cooperation could be an effective solution to tackle these problems amid a global economic slowdown.

Surakiat Sathirathai, coordinator with the Asia Cooperation Dialogue and Thai minister of foreign affairs, said that Asian countries and regions should take advantage of the diversity in natural environments and cultural heritage to cooperate over regional tourism. He also held that the forum mechanism would help promote Asian tourism as a whole.

Myra P. Gunawan, deputy chairman for tourism affairs of the Indonesia Culture and Tourism Board, noted that the members of the Association of Southeast Asian Nations (ASEAN) had agreed to promote ASEAN as a single tourist destination so as to help increase their share of the world tourism market.

The Sept. 11 terror attacks, the recent Bali bombing and other terrorist assaults had produced lingering negative impacts on tourism, which greatly concerned all the participants.

Meanwhile, Vietnamese Deputy Prime Minister Vu Khoan cited stability as a prime factor to the fast growth of Asian tourism, which called for joint efforts by all parties concerned and cooperation based on mutual respect.

Participants also reached consensus on a number of ideas and envisages concerning specific cooperation. Several delegates believed that it should start with information sharing and the training of professionals.

Australian and Chinese tourism experts have already launched training programs for senior tourism executives for some countries and regions at the forum.

As the host country, China has always valued tourism exchanges and mutually beneficial cooperation with other Asian countries and regions. Of the 11.23 million overseas arrivals to China in 2001, 62 percent of the travelers came from across Asia. The destinations for Chinese outbound travelers were also mainly Asian.

He Guangwei, director of the China National Tourism Administration (CNTA) said, "China and Asian countries and regions are reciprocal destinations and sources for international tourism, forming a dual-track and interactive framework for tourist cooperation."

Guilin, the picturesque host city, epitomizes in a concentrated way the substantial achievements China's tourist industry has scored in sustainable tourism. Delegates to the forum spoke highly of the prosperous development in Chinese tourism and are convinced that the forum would further enhance China's image as a safe and sound tourist destination.

Meanwhile, Asia is the fastest-growing region in world tourism. With the concerted efforts of all parties, Asia's fast-developing tourism can retain the title.

As Chen Jinhua, vice-chairman of the National Committee of the Chinese People's Political Consultative Conference said, the successful convocation of the forum ushered in a new phase of regional cooperation for Asian tourism and injected a new impetus for regional prosperity and development.

IMPORTANCE OF TOURISM

The importance of tourism had been recognized since early days of SAARC. The Leaders during the Second Summit held at Bangalore in 1986 underlined that concrete steps should be taken to facilitate tourism in the region. A Technical Committee on Tourism was created in 1991. During the First Meeting of the Technical Committee on Tourism held in Colombo in October 1991, an Action Plan on Tourism was formulated.

First Meeting of the SAARC Tourism Ministers was held in Colombo in September 1997. It adopted Colombo Resolution and approved a number of important activities. In 1999, the task of promoting tourism was assigned to the SAARC Chamber of Commerce & Industry (SCCI) Tourism Council.

The Twenty-fourth Session of the Council of Ministers (Islamabad, 2-3 January 2004) approved establishment of the Working Group on Tourism. The First Meeting was held in Colombo in August 2004. The Working Group on Tourism prepared Plan of Activities which includes promotion of SAARC as a common tourist destination, to encourage private sector in promoting regional cooperation in tourism, human resource development, promotion of South Asia identity through tourism, cultural and eco-tourism development. The Working Group was authorized to periodically review implementation of this Action Plan.

During the Thirteenth Summit (Dhaka, 12-13 November 2005), the Leaders stressed that continued efforts would be made by the Member States at all levels to promote people-to-people contact by facilitating travel among SAARC countries, promotion of youth exchanges in culture and sports, promotion of intra-SAARC tourism, establishment of linkages among professional bodies and through adoption of other concrete measures. They decided to launch 2006 as "South Asia Tourism Year." They directed their Ministers for Tourism to meet at an early date and elaborate a plan of activities to be undertaken during the year 2006.

The Tourism Ministers who met at Cox's Bazar (Bangladesh) in May 2006, adopted the Cox's Bazar SAARC Action Plan on Tourism.

Second Meeting of the Working Group on Tourism, held in Colombo on 3-4 July 2006, recommended that for promoting SAARC as common tourist destination (i) national airlines may use SAARC logo on aircrafts and other promotional brochures; (ii) national airlines may also use SAARC flag with their own flag as well as national flags at their offices and (iii) the Head of Mission representing the Chair of SAARC will organize special events in celebration of SAARC Charter Day on 8 December, with focus on promoting tourism.

In the Fourteenth Summit the Heads of State or Government while noting the cultural and social ties among the SAARC countries, based on common history and geography, reiterated that the future of peoples of South Asia is interlinked. They stressed the importance of people-to-people contact as a key constituent in regional connectivity. They acknowledged the importance of intra-regional tourism and increased exchanges, particularly among the youth, civil society, and parliamentarians. They agreed to take measures to charge nationals of SAARC Member States fees for entry into archeological and heritage sites as applicable to their own nationals.

The Heads of State or Government during the Fifteenth Summit underscored the vital contribution that tourism could afford to the economic development of the SAARC region. They agreed to make every effort to implement the comprehensive action plan adopted by the Second Ministerial Meeting held at Cox's Bazaar, Bangladesh. These efforts would include facilitating the movement of people through improved travel infrastructure and air, sea and land connectivity among the SAARC countries, collaboration in human resource development and the promotion of SAARC as a common destination through public-private partnerships and joint campaigns.

The Working Group in its Third Meeting held in Colombo in April 2009 reviewed the status of implementation of the Summit directives, SAARC Action Plan on tourism, and various decisions taken by the Ministerial and Working Group Meetings. It also finalized a list of activities to be undertaken during the year 2009-10 for tourism promotion among the SAARC countries.

REGIONAL COOPERATION AND RURAL TOURISM IN CROATIA

Rural tourism in Croatia is an important factor in the activation and sustainable development of rural areas, which helps to preserve the local identity, tradition and customs, protecting thus the environment, strengthening the indigenous, traditional and organic production, and supporting the development of rural areas based on sustainable development. In Croatia, rural tourism is in its initial phase and presents a great potential which has not been given enough attention so far.

In Croatia, it is increasingly understood that sustainable development of rural areas is the optimal development solution. Croatian rural areas can be developed only by way of sustainable development. In this sense, the role of the central government is essential, primarily by investing the capital investments in infrastructure, with appropriate legislative enactments. Also, the NGOs should have an important role in promoting the idea of sustainable development through monitoring and constructive guidance.

Croatia has a significant and numerous natural and socio-cultural resource bases for tourism development in all its regions, not only in the maritime ones. However, is this resource base sufficiently and properly used, and is there an appropriate and feasible strategy for the development of rural tourism and other activities related to sustainable development of rural areas in Croatia? The question which arises is whether agriculture and tourism are Croatia's basic development opportunities.

In addition, the study provides an overview and analysis of rural tourism in Europe, its key international organizations and national associations as well as their importance for the sustainable development of European countries. It also presents the European examples of successful models of rural tourism development, interprets some new rural tourism products in Europe – didactic farms and open-air museums, and, finally, explains the Leader Plus initiative, financed by the European Union Structural Funds. Particular attention was given to the possibilities and ways as to how to apply and use the presented European experiences, particularly those relating to the use of Structural Funds and European Union programs designed for rural tourism, as well as to the examples of good practice in the development of rural tourism in Croatia on the threshold of its accession to the European Union.

It may be of particular use to the local population in improving the rural environment, preserving the tradition and landscape, and bringing them closer to the increasing number of tourists. This study represents a valuable contribution to the scientific research of rural tourism in Croatia, and can serve as an appropriate basis for all future research of this topic. Also, it draws attention to the importance of rural tourism in Croatia as well as to the need for more specific involvement of the central government in its further development in terms of elaborating a national program or strategy for the development of rural tourism as one of Croatia's key components of sustainable development.

The importance of rural tourism is primarily reflected in the very important interaction between agricultural production, production of traditional products, presentation of traditions, traditional gastronomy and tourist services, or the use of existing resources. Rural tourism development is based on sustainable development. It is visible in the revitalization of the existing traditional construction and heritage, which are being given a new purpose – a touristic one. Rural tourism, in a completely different way, tries to unite, restore and organize the territory. There is no need to build new capacity, but, rather, rural tourism development is faced with the challenge as to how to use the existing structures in the best and most effective way.

A complete reconstruction, evaluation and protection of touristic resources as well as the creation of an integrated touristic product are associated with the program of revitalization of rural areas through the development and branding of rural tourism destinations and rural tourism. Particularly tourism in the framework of touristic farms must be viewed as an essential component of the overall sustainable development.

Although rural tourism in Croatia is not given the necessary importance, due to the meaning it has in the creation of new values in rural areas, recently we are witnessing an increase in the interest of public administration, local governments, institutions and individual entrepreneurs in rural areas for the development and promotion of that activity. However, further development, education, financing, promotion and cooperation are needed on different levels.

It is therefore necessary to encourage stronger collaboration of all relevant institutions (state administration, regional and local governments, tourist boards' system, regional development agencies, scientific and professional institutions, trade associations) with the purpose of initiating joint activities to develop rural tourism and elaborate a national program (strategy) for the development of rural areas and Croatian tourism, as well as to encourage cooperation of touristic farms and other rural entrepreneurs in rural tourism, by way of strengthening the existing and establishing new associations and cooperatives.

In Croatia's rural areas, the relationship between nature and the rural population is to a great extent preserved, which, mostly independently, develop a sense of tourism with their own enthusiasm and basically modest tourist knowledge. Due to that, in the development of tourism in the rural areas in Croatia, residents of particular regions cooperate with and consult tourist and local political structures. Together, with their initiatives and self-organization, they form a vision of tourism according to which they activate their own economic potential. Tourist development of rural areas requires the coexistence with traditional culture with optimal utilization of tourist diversity.

During the revitalization of rural areas it is necessary to increase the population, especially the return of those who have migrated to the cities and abroad. Other settlers should not numerically exceed the critical level of relations to the detriment of the local population, nor the number of positions in local government and the economy. It is due to the fact that local people are the ones who give the uniqueness and particularity of tradition and lifestyle, while all others must acclimatize emotionally with rural areas.

Sustainable development of Croatian rural areas should follow the traditional way of life in them. We should not witness the situation when the culture of farmers is being presented to the tourists, while they actually do not exist. It should, therefore, continue the tradition and further enrich it. Offer should be organized in rural areas in small or larger settlements with amenities such as hunting, fishing, biking, hiking, mountaineering, field cultivating, harvesting, and the like.

Therefore, through sustainable rural development more problems should be determined and questions answered, such as: how to protect the so far preserved area, what are the benefits of development of specific regions, which are the limits of development of specific regions, which role in the development does the state administration and local government have, should the development be initiated on the cultural, historical and economic recognition or is there a need to create some new assumptions, how to create a development that itself will not lead to collapse, and other.

A reasonable strategy for rural development in Croatia should avoid the destiny of the Mediterranean developed countries, whose original environment is so destroyed that they became undesirable for local inhabitants and tourists. Sustainable development of Croatian rural areas must be dealt with far-reaching strategy assessment, which will prevent its negative impacts.

Touristic destinations must retain authenticity, remain faithful to its cultural traditions and on these grounds draw strength for development. Promotion of sustainable cultural development is a condition of keeping the local cultural particularities. Touristic stakeholders must identify and promote their local cultural values, and changes should not take place at the expense of inherited values.

The main objective of tourism in rural areas in Croatia must be to improve the quality of life and prevent depopulation, preferably by policy of small steps, starting from demand requirements. Excessive investments in tourism, except in infrastructure, have devastating effect on the area and population. Future development policy for each area must be unique and avoid general ways of overall development of Croatian rural areas.

Common to this approach is that population realizes the state of social and economic security as well as equal status in regard to urban residents. For every rural region in Croatia the concept of development with the requirement of preserving its original features, nature and cultural heritage should be determined.

15 New Direction in Rural Tourism

The main thrust is that as affluent retirees and other wealthy buyers purchase second homes on remote areas, they bring with them demand for interior-design studios, spas and organic supermarkets. These shops are now popping up in these areas. It's a dramatic change. According to some sociologists, some residents of these areas consider this trend the most significant change to their areas since the interstate highways first came through.

Of course, such change has its good and bad sides. On the positive side, the new shops are a nice amenity for the residents of these rural areas. On the negative, the influx of wealthy second-home buyers can drive up property values so high that longtime residents of an area can no longer afford to live there.

The definition of Rural Community Tourism has an inner circle of planned tourist sustainability experiences integrated in a rural environment. These experiences are developed by the locals, organized to benefit of the community.

According to some experts, rural tourism is more than that. Rural tourism is a bunch of activities which main goal is to improve the quality of life for those who develop these kinds of projects. Its autochthonous sense allows the 100% income to stay in the family or the community that uses this idea.

Costa Rica as a rural country in essence grew in this matter thanks to our famer's determination. It is this reason that does not let in any way to forget our roots. Based on recovering the history, traditions and customs Rural Tourism generates employment and a better life because the business is the most important for the developers and all people involve.

Rural Tourism needs more support from those who face the business enterprises and those who take the decision to promote Costa Rica. This can be done through a deeper development that intensifies the support and participation of the different activities that show the value of Rural Tourism.

With the creation of the new law "Ley de Fomento al Turismo Rural Comunitario" (Rural Community Tourism Encouragement Law) the National Chamber of Rural Community Tourism was created in order to impulse this sector.

The big role of the Rural Community Tourism now is how it is facing the economic isolation. The impulse that Rural Tourism gives to business skill development, the capacity to stop migration from the country to the city, the high value of the local culture, the development of new infrastructure, the promotion of natural resources conservation, among others are the main reasons to comprehend the importance of this segment in the tourism sector.

We congratulate all public or private initiative that pretends to strengthen this area, because all the economical problems and the recession is when the businesspeople use all their capacity in creativity and innovation to make the hard times softer, with the creation of new products to attract not only different kinds of tourists, but to continue in the worldwide lead that we have had over the years.

The contribution of the businesspeople and community leaders has been very important. There is no doubt that we will have great news from Rural Community Tourism in the years to come.The recent non-metropolitan turnaround in the USA has resulted in population migration from large cities to small towns and countryside. The marketing opportunity presented to rural tourism comes with significant challenges for its sustainability.

The focus of extant literature on sustainability has been more on the environmental and socio-cultural protection of the intrinsic qualities in the countryside, but less on the economic viability and marketing feasibility of rural tourism. The understanding of rural tourists has particularly been overlooked.

This chapter examined the relationship between population migration at tourist origins and tourist arrivals from these origins to a rural destination. Through a conceptual application of gravity model, the study found that population migration exerted a significant effect on tourist arrivals. The study also revealed that the demographic variable of gender affected the dynamics of the relationship, suggesting that demographic information of migrants at tourist origins can offer richer marketing intelligence for rural destinations. The study's findings highlight the importance for rural communities to understand population migration at source markets, and provide a scientific tool to predict migration-induced tourist demand to rural destinations.

LANDSCAPES AND TRADITIONS

The countryside and mountains have preserved their landscapes and their traditions. But although green tourism represents a very real opportunity for Romania, its growth threatens the authenticity of unique regions such as Maramures.

The tiny mountainous region of Maramures, neighbouring the Ukraine in northern Transylvania, is sometimes presented as the Shangri-La of all that is quintessentially Romanian. But the mythical Romanian peasant is having a hard time in a country that remains predominantly agricultural as it joins the European Union.

Far from the mass tourism of the Black Sea coast or the castles that are said to have been the home of Dracula, this green region with its deep-rooted traditions has seen the arrival of a quite separate race: the post-modern tourist, explains Raluca Nagy. "Ten years ago, these tourists discovered Prague; today they have their sights on Bucharest or Sofia." She adds, "The ethno tourist is not interested in getting a suntan, but in discovering something new, and is fascinated and attracted by all that is different."

She goes on, "The picture-book landscape of Maramures and the myth of the true Romania, somewhat erroneous given a history marked by the arrival of the Hungarians and Ukrainians, have made this region a success. In just a few years, 'friendly' tourism based on traditional hospitality has given way to a more commercial relationship."

Nagy adds, "The people of Maramures, often part-time farmers, have turned to rural tourism. Some of them, those who work abroad, have even put up new buildings to welcome the visitors in greater comfort than the traditional wooden houses. The development of these sanitized *pensiuni* is, however, a threat to the very thing that attracts the tourist to Maramures: its authenticity. It could even risk disappearing altogether."

Yet despite all this, green tourism remains an asset for Romania. As Nagy puts it, "No other country in Europe has more variety to offer the tourist, but it is a potential that must be used intelligently."

RURAL DEVELOPMENT FUNDS

Small towns in the United States run on CDBG and USDA Rural Development funds and they are about to be drastically cut according to news reports both national and local. Attend any rural community meeting discussing how to build a new, community center, or upgrade a small town water system, and the first solution you'll hear is, "Get a grant to pay for that."

Reading the latest news, I have a huge concern: These rural development and CDBG grants are the life's blood for struggling rural communities. And our biggest competitors for this money are urban areas.

Who has the most leverage when it comes to getting a slice of the new, much smaller pie? A major metropolitan area with a ton of voters, or a small town of 3000 in a rural county with a total voting block of less than 50,000?

Our major voices in this huge debate are the regional rural economic development organizations and RC&D's that have our best interests at heart and their own survival at stake.

They use this money to keep their doors open so they can help rural business owners and small towns. They pass it through to us in the form of microloans, business development services and community development projects. And they need our help.

The first big debate which is being considered right now is about clarifying what is "rural." It seems obvious right? You know it when you see it, right? Not so.

How about this. According to this post in the Daily Yonder, "Define Rural before You Budget for It," you're looking at a picture of an urban center. Yup, the Grand Canyon is "metro" according to federal use of county demographics. Part of it is in populous Coconino County!

With battles ahead for the bits of federal assistance that is allowing many rural communities to continue to exist, we need to do two things immediately:

1. Become aware of all the local and regional rural economic development organizations that serve your rural area, find out what they do and contact your congressmen and legislators to express your support of their efforts.

2. Get involved with new efforts to clarify a definition of rural. Read the article in the Daily Yonder to more fully understand the complexity of what would seem to be a simple thing.

Why is this so important? A new Farm Bill will be debated soon in Congress, with the existing Farm Bill due to expire in 2012. Having a clearer, non-agricultural definition of rural will mean that your small town won't be need to compete with big agribusinesses like Archers Daniels Midland (ADM) for grants and subsidies in that gigantic bill.

Remember the next time you hear someone in your small town say "We can get a grant for that" exactly where that grant money comes from, and how easily it could become a thing of the past.

Rural Development

Rural development in general is used to denote the actions and initiatives taken to improve the standard of living in non-Urban neighbourhoods, countryside, and remote villages. These communities can be exemplified with a low ratio of inhabitants to open space. Agricultural activities may be prominent in this case whereas economic activities would relate to the primary sector, production of food stuffs and raw materials.

Rural development actions mostly aim at the social and economic development of the areas. These programs are usually top-down from the local or regional authorities, regional development agencies, NGOs, national governments or international development organizations. But then, local populations can also bring about endogenous initiatives for development. The term is not limited to the issues for developing countries. In fact many of the developed countries have very active rural development programs.The main aim of the rural government policy is to develop the undeveloped villages.

Vacation Property

Vacation property is a niche in the real estate market dealing with residences used for holiday vacations (e.g. beach house). In the United Kingdom this type of property is usually termed a *holiday home*, in Australia, a *holiday house/home*, or *weekender*, in New Zealand, a *bach* or *crib*. In the United States the most common designation is *second home*.

A second home or vacation home can be a home owner's asset as renting it could provide additional income. Many vacationers are opting for a single family residence that they can rent on a nightly or weekly basis. In many cases the savings for them are significant compared to hotels or vacation packages. For owners it can be as rewarding as paying the mortgage. As people begin to realize this trend vacation type properties are becoming popular not only for existing homes but also for building one.

Wales

Holiday homes and second homes comprise 14% of the housing stock in Snowdonia, Wales, compared to the figure of 1% for the whole of Wales. Only in Gwynedd has the council has put in place measures to control the number of holiday homes. But they only control new developments, by withholding permission where consent is likely to raise the figure in any community above 10%, they do not stop anyone from buying a holiday home.

England

The number in Cornwall and the Isles of Scilly was calculated to be 5.6% in 2004 and 2006, this is the region which has the highest number of second homes in England. Within a year alone, between 2004 and 2005, the percentage of holiday/second homes in England increased by 3.3%.

There were 29,299 holiday/summer homes in Scotland on the 2001 Scottish Census, which accounted for 1.3% of Scotland's housing stock. This figure was 19,756 in 1981, but the majority of the increase occurred during the 1990s. The greatest increase was seen in urban areas, contrary to the usual trends, and increased especially in Edinburgh and Aberdeen. But the majority of holiday/ second homes are still to be found in rural areas, notably, 47% of these are to be found in the remote rural areas, where one in every eight house is a holiday or second home.

France

The figure in France is also fairly high: approximately 10% of all the housing stock is a holiday or second home, but the majority of these are owned by French. There are approximately 300,000 homes, or 1% of the total housing stock which are the property of owners from abroad. Of this percentage 28% are owned by British owners, 14% Italian, 10% Belgian, 8% Dutch, 3% Spanish and 3% American.

In 2000, 3,578,718, or 3.09% of the United States' housing stock, were holiday or second homes, compared with 2.66% in

1990, and 1.87% in 1980. 26% of all these are located in the north-eastern states, with approximately 250,199 (7% of all the second homes in the U.S.) located in New York, and Maine having the largest percentage of its housing stock as second homes.

COSTS AND EFFECTS

Second home and holiday home owners used to be able to claim discounts in their council tax in the United Kingdom, as the property is vacant for much of the year. This is no longer true in many counties, including Carmarthenshire; if the property is empty (but furnished) no discount is permitted and the owner will be liable to pay the tax in full. But, In Cornwall, since 2004 second home owners can claim a 10% discount in their counciltax. Prior to 2004, they could claim a 50% discount in Cornwall, they are still able to claim 50% in many other areas in England.

The Welsh movement, Cymuned, promote the principle that owners of holiday homes should pay double the standard rate of council tax, as they do not otherwise invest in the local community. Testimony of this is t be seen in a report on the effect of holiday homes in Scotland, which found that those who went on holiday to Scotland spent an average of £57 a day, in comparison to just £32 a day spent by those visiting their holiday or second homes.

Furnished holiday lettings offer other tax relief providing certain conditions are met. The current conditions are:

- It should be available for commercial letting to the public for a total of 140 days in the 12 month period.
- It must be let for at least 70 days in the 12 month period. (Where more than one qualifying property is held, it is possible to average the number of days all properties are let in total in order to meet this condition.)
- The total periods of long term occupation may not exceed 155 days during the 12 month period.

A proposed change to UK law due April 2011 will increase the minimum time a property must be available for let in order to qualify as a furnished holiday letting. Owners of holiday homes will occasionally move to their second homes permanently upon retirement, this can be a threat to the culture of an area, especially in Wales where the influx of non-Welsh speakers effects the percentage of Welsh speakers in the area and reduces the use of Welsh in everyday life. Hundreds of second homes were burnt between 1979 and the mid-1990s as a part of a campaign by nationalist movement Meibion Glyndur to protect the indigenous language and culture.

The rapid development of the Internet and technologies such as telephony and personal digital assistants that allow people to work from home since circa 1995 has blurred the division between vacation property and a primary residence. Some business people, including the British entrepreneur Richard Branson, use their luxury real estate for both business and leisure purposes.Many internet services have developed to connect short term rental customers with owners or brokers of vacation properties.

16 RURAL TOURISM AND SUSTAINABILITY

The Sustainable Rural Tourism programme aims to attract more than 300,000 extra overnight visitors into the region each year. Its six projects will focus on the opportunities for tourists - to the benefit of south west businesses and residents - to make the most of the South West Coast Path, Cornish Mining World Heritage site, inland water bodies, cycle & multi-use trails and the natural habitat.

More than £14 million is being provided by a grant from the Rural Development Programme for England (RDPE), with a further £4 million contributed by the private sector and the organisations leading delivery of the projects. Around half of the funding will be spent in Cornwall, although the split within individual projects varies.

The six projects are:

- **1 South West** - A partnership led by the Forestry Commission will create easy access trail hubs to develop South West England as a world-class region for adventurous off-road cycling. With some trails suitable for absolute beginners, the hubs will enable enjoyable cycling activity throughout the year. This work will be enhanced through improved information for off-road cycling across the region, providing a platform for further development.

- **Outdoor & Active** - A partnership led by the South West Lakes Trust, and involving the Cotswold Water Park Trust and the Environment Agency, it aims to develop waterside recreation - ranging from wildlife watching to regional racing and canoe safaris - at six interlinked hubs situated at reservoirs and lakes across the region.
- **Unlocking our Coastal Heritage** - A partnership led by the South West Coast Path Team to conserve, enhance and interpret 30 sites along the South West Coast Path National Trail. It aims to improve the quality of the visitor experience and increase the economic benefits to the associated tourism industry.
- **Discover the Extraordinary Project** - The Cornish Mining World Heritage Site has ambitious plans for developing the quality and appeal of the World Heritage mining landscape and attractions in Cornwall and West Devon.
- **Country Sports South West** - A partnership between the British Association for Shooting and Conservation and Westcountry Rivers Trust will be looking to develop the full potential of the region's country sports market and its related supporting industries.
- **TRAC (Tourism and Rural Access in Cornwall)** - Cornwall Council is working with businesses to develop links between the Camel and Tarka multi-use trails, particularly on the Devon and Cornwall border, to help diversify tourism facilities and interest to areas in the less traditional tourist 'hotspots'.

INTEGRATED RURAL DEVELOPMENT PROGRAM (IRDP)

The Integrated Rural Development Programme is a rural development program of the Government of India launched in Financial Year 1978 and extended throughout India by 1980. It is a self-employment program intended to raise the income-generation capacity of target groups among the poor. The aim is to raise recipients above the poverty line by providing substantial opportunities for self-employment.

During the 7th five year plan, the total expenditure under the program was Rs 33.2 million, and Rs 53.7 million of term credit was mobilized. Some 13 million new families participated, bringing total coverage under the program to more than 18 million families. These development programs have played an important role in increased agricultural production by educating farmers and providing them with financial and other inputs to increase yields.

The objective of IRDP is to enable identified rural poor families to cross the poverty line by providing productive assets and inputs to the target groups. The assets which could be in primary, secondary or tertiary sector are provided through financial assistance in the form of subsidy by the government and term credit advanced by financial institutions. The program is implemented in all the blocks in the country as a centrally sponsored scheme funded on 50:50 basis by the Centre and State. The Scheme is merged with another Scheme named swarnjayanti gram swarozgar yojana (SGSY) since 1April, 1999.

Sustainable Living

Sustainable living is fundamentally the application of sustainability to lifestyle choice and decisions. Sustainability itself is expressed as meeting present ecological, societal, and economical needs without compromising these factors for future generations Sustainable living can therefore be described as living within the innate carrying capacities defined by these factors.

Sustainable design and sustainable development are critical factors to sustainable living. Sustainable design encompasses the development of appropriate technology, which is a staple of sustainable living practices. Sustainable development in turn is the use of these technologies in infrastructure. Sustainable architecture and agriculture are the most common examples of this practice.

Sustainable living is a lifestyle that attempts to reduce an individual's or society's use of the Earth's natural resource and his/her own resources. Practitioners of sustainable living often attempt to reduce their carbon footprint by altering methods of transportation, energy consumption and diet. Proponents of sustainable living aim to conduct their lives in manners that are consistent with sustainability, in natural balance and respectful of humanity's symbiotic relationship with the Earth's natural ecology and cycles. The practice and general philosophy of ecological living is highly interrelated with the overall principles of sustainable development.

Organic Farming

Purchasing and supporting organic products is another fundamental contribution to sustainable living. Organic farming is a rapidly emerging trend in the food industry and in the web of sustainability. According to the USDA National Organic Standards Board (NOSB), organic agriculture is defined as "an ecological production management system that promotes and enhances biodiversity, biological cycles, and soil biological activity. It is based on minimal use of off-farm inputs and on management practices that restore, maintain, or enhance ecological harmony.

The primary goal of organic agriculture is to optimize the health and productivity of interdependent communities of soil life, plants, animals and people." Upon sustaining these goals, organic agriculture uses techniques such as crop rotation, permaculture, compost, green manure and biological pest control.

In addition, organic farming prohibits or strictly limits the use of manufactured fertilizers and pesticides, plant growth regulators such as hormones, livestock antibiotics, food additives and genetically modified organisms. Organically farmed products include vegetables, fruit, grains, herbs, meat, dairy, eggs, fibers, and flowers. See organic certification for more information.

Sustainable landscaping

Sustainable landscaping encompasses a variety of practices that have developed in response to environmental issues. These practices are used in every phase of landscaping, including design, construction, implementation and management of residential and commercial landscapes.

Some of the effects of non-sustainable practices are: Threats to health, well-being and even survival of humans and other life forms and their habitats; sedimentation of surface waters caused by stormwater runoff; chemical pollutants in drinking water caused by pesticide runoff; health problems caused by toxic fertilizers, toxic pesticides, improper use, handling, storage and disposal of pesticides; air and noise pollution caused by landscape equipment; and over-use of limited natural resources.

Sustainable landscaping solutions

Some of the solutions being developed are:

- Reduction of stormwater run-off through the use of bio-swales, rain gardens and green roofs and walls.
- Reduction of water use in landscapes through design of water-wise garden techniques (sometimes known as xeriscaping™)
- Bio-filtering of wastes through constructed wetlands
- Landscape irrigation using water from showers and sinks, known as gray water
- Integrated Pest Management techniques for pest control
- Creating and enhancing wildlife habitat in urban environments
- Energy-efficient landscape design in the form of proper placement and selection of shade trees and creation of wind breaks
- Permeable paving materials to reduce stormwater run-off and allow rain water to infiltrate into the ground and replenish groundwater rather than run into surface water

- Use of sustainably harvested wood, composite wood products for decking and other landscape projects, as well as use of plastic lumber
- Recycling of products, such as glass, rubber from tires and other materials to create landscape products such as paving stones, mulch and other materials
- Soil management techniques, including composting kitchen and yard wastes, to maintain and enhance healthy soil that supports a diversity of soil life
- Integration and adoption of renewable energy, including solar-powered landscape lighting

A sustainable landscape is designed to be both attractive and in balance with the local climate and environment and it should require minimal resource inputs. Thus, the design must be "functional, cost-efficient, visually pleasing, environmentally friendly and maintainable" As part of the concept called sustainable development it pays close attention to the preservation of limited and costly resources, reducing waste and preventing air, water and soil pollution.

Also, compost, fertilization, grass cycling, pest control measures that avoid or minimize the use of chemicals, integrated pest management, using the right plant in the right place, appropriate use of turf, irrigation efficiency and xeriscaping or water-wise gardening are all components of sustainable landscaping.

Benefits

The geographic location can determine what is sustainable due to differences in precipitation and temperature. For example, the California Waste Management Board emphasizes the link between minimizing environmental damage and maximizing one's bottom line of urban commercial landscaping companies. In California, the benefits of landscapes often do not outweigh the cost of inputs like water and labor. However, using appropriately selected and properly sited plants may help to ensure that maintenance costs are lower than they otherwise would be due to reduced chemical and water inputs.

Programs

There are several programs in place that are open to participation by various groups. For example, the Audubon Cooperative Sanctuary Program for Golf Courses, the Audubon Green Neighborhoods™ Program and the National Wildlife Federation's Backyard Habitat™ Program to name a few.

The Sustainable Sites Initiative, the cooperative effort between the American Society of Landscape Architects, the Lady Bird Johnson Wildflower Center and the United States Botanic Garden, began in 2005 and will provide a points-based certification for landscapes, similar to the LEED program for buildings operated by the Green Building Council. The Sustainable Sites Initiative now has a document titled Guidelines and Performance Benchmarks. The credit system is expected to be completed in 2011.

Proper Design

The primary step to landscape design is to do a "sustainability audit". This is similar to a landscape site analysis that is typically performed by landscape designers at the beginning of the design process. Factors such as lot size, house size, local covenants and budgets should be considered. The steps to design include a base plan, site inventory and analysis, construction documents, implementation and maintenance. Other considerations include orientation to the sun, soil type, slopes, location of utility lines and planned usage.

Earthworms, microbes and other soil flora and fauna feast on such organic matter when provided adequate nitrogen and proper temperatures and moisture. The ideal size for a compost pile or bin is one cubic yard (3' x 3' x 3'). It should be placed in a partly shady location to avoid intense sun and drying out, as this will delay the decomposition process.

The pile heats up during the decomposition process, then cools as material is transformed, this is a good time to turn the pile, so that undecomposed materials on the periphery of the pile can be moved to the center to complete the process. With adequate moisture, nitrogen, proper temperature and correct timing of turning the pile, compost can be made in about a 30-day period. Left alone this pocess will still occur, but may take three to four months under less-than-ideal conditions.

Compost can be added as an amendment to poorly draining soil, as a fertilizer on flower and vegetable beds, to fruit trees or used as a potting soil for potted plants. Trimmings from lawns, trees and shrubs from a large landscape site can be used as feedstock for on-site composting. Reusing on-site organic materials will decrease the need for purchasing other soil additives.

Irrigation

Using mulch is a great way to reduce water loss due to evaporation, reduce weeds, minimize erosion, dust and mud problems. Mulch will also add nutrients to the soil when it decomposes. Grass cycling turf areas (using mulching mowers that leave grass clippings on the lawn) will also decrease the amount of fertilizer needed, reduce landfill waste and reduce costs of disposal.

A common recommendation is to adding 2-4 inches of mulch in flower beds and under trees away from the trunk. Mulch should be applied under trees to the dripline (extension of the branches) in lieu of flowers, hostas, turf or other plants that are often planted there. This practice of planting under trees is detrimental to tree roots, especially when such plants are irrigated to an excessive level that harms the tree.

The practice of xeriscaping or water-wise gardening suggests that placing plants with similar water demands together will save time and low-water or drought tolerant plants would be a smart initial consideration.

A homeowner may consider consulting an accredited irrigation technician/auditor and obtain a water audit of current systems. In the event that the situation is difficult to manage, drip or sub-surface irrigation may be most effective. If the system has been in use for over five years, upgrading to evapotranspiration (ET) controllers, soil sensors and refined control panels will improvc the system. Oftentimes irrigation heads are in need of readjustment to avoid sprinkling on sidewalks or streets. Business owners may consider developing watering schedules based on historical or actual weather data and soil probes to monitor soil moisture prior to watering.

BUILDING MATERIALS

When deciding what kind of building materials to put on a site it is important to recycle as often as possible. Reusing old bricks from sidewalks as patio pavers is one way to provide an aesthetic appeal to an area while reducing what goes to the landfill.

But it is also important to be careful about what materials you use, especially if you plan to grow food crops of any kind. Old telephone poles and railroad ties have usually been treated with a substance called creosote that can leach into the soils and make any food grown there toxic enough to cause harm to anyone that eats it. In general, you should avoid any kind of treated material, especially wood, that could leach into the soil with rain.

The Forest Stewardship Council (http://www.fscus.org/) was formed in 1993 "to change the dialogue about and the practice of sustainable forestry worldwide." Sustainably harvested lumber - also called certified wood is now available, in which ecological, economic and social factors are integrated into the management of trees used for lumber. A chain of custody document is used in the certification process.

PLANTING SELECTION

One important part of sustainable landscaping is plant selection. Most of what makes a landscape unsustainable is the amount of inputs required to grow a non-native plant on it. What this means is that a local plant, which has adapted to local climate conditions will require less work on the part of some other agent to flourish. For example, it does not make sense to grow tomatoes in Arizona because there is not enough natural rainfall for them to survive without constant watering. Instead, drought tolerant plants like succulents and cacti are better suited to survive. Also, by choosing native plants, one can avoid certain problems with insects and pests because these plants will also be adapted to deal with any local invader. The bottom line is that by choosing the right kind of local plants, a great deal of money can be saved on amendment costs, pest control and watering.

Plants used as windbreaks can save up to 30% on heating costs in winter. They also help with shading a residence or commercial building in summer, create cool air through evapo-transpiration and can cool hardscaped areas such as driveways and sidewalks.

A house surrounded by local trees or bushes enjoys multiple benefits. Plants release water vapor in the air through transpiration and water has the ability to reduce temperature extremes in the areas near it (as it boasts very high heat capacity). The larger and more leafy the plant, the most water vapor it produces. Additionally, the presence of trees is crucial in the creation of stable, healthy and productive ecosystems (such as forests). In fact this is an important principle of permaculture.

If the surrounding trees are chosen to produce edible fruit they can provide a sustainable food source for the occupants of the house. Even if some are fairly demanding (especially in the summer), irrigation is an excellent end-use option in greywater recycling and rainwater harvesting systems, and a composting toilet can cover (at least) some of the nutrient requirements. Research suggests that diluted human urine might be as effective as chemical fertilizers. It must be noted that not all fruit trees are suitable for greywater irrigation, as reclaimed greywater is typically of high pH and acidophile plants don't do well in alkaline environments.

An intelligent choice for direct energy conservation would be the placement of broadleaf deciduous trees near the east, west and optionally north-facing walls of the house. Such selection provides shading in the summer while permitting large amounts of heat-carrying solar radiation to strike the house in the winter. The trees are to be placed as closely as possible to the house walls but no closer than 1 meter - otherwise the roots can cause substantial foundation damage. A sustainable house will most likely be equipped with south-facing (north-facing in the S. hemisphere) photovoltaic panels and a large, south-facing glazing as a result of passive solar heating design. As the efficiency of both systems is very sensitive to shading, experts suggest the complete absence of trees near the south side.

Another intelligent choice would be that of a dense vegetative fence composed of evergreens (e.g. conifers) near that side from which cold continental winds blow (usually north in the N. hemisphere) and also that side from which the prevailing winds blow (west in temperate regions of both hemispheres). Since north winds are most cold and westerlies blow most often, such choice creates an effective winter windbarrier that prevents very low temperatures outside the house and reduces air infiltration towards the inside. Calculations show that placing the windbrake at a distance twice the height of the trees can reduce the wind velocity by 75%. It then follows that, with some planning, both arrangements (deciduous and evergreen) can be applied simultaneously.

It must be noted that the above vegetative arrangements come with two disadvantages. Firstly, they minimize air circulation in summer (although in many climates heating is more important and costly than cooling) and, secondly, they may affect the efficiency of photovoltaic panels, thus prompting the need for a shading analysis. However, it has been estimated that if both arrangements are applied properly, they can reduce the overall house energy usage by up to 22%.

Plant Health

Pest Problems Maintaining plant health will eliminate most pest problems. It is best to start with pest-free plant materials and supplies and close inspection of the plant upon purchase is also

Although some farms did sell local products (e.g. farm produce, delicacies and handicrafts), this was not usually an important source of income. According to the survey, the majority of revenues were generated by serving meals (46%), followed by selling farm products (18%), accommodation (12%), selling local specialities (10%) and others (14%).

FARM INNS

Farm inns are small-scale accomodation. A few rooms in farmhouses are renovated and made available to tourists. Farm inns are located near beautiful scenery or historic sites. To attract more tourists, it is recommended that at least five farmhouses in any one village should establish a farm inn. Not all provide meals, whereas nearly all tourism farms provide cooked meals. The survey showed that farm inns also shared a number of problems.

Facilities

The facilities of most farm inns are not yet of a very high standard. Many of the houses are old and poorly maintained. Many do not have a toilet and shower for the exclusive use of guests. Out of 503 inns, 154 (31%) did not have an independent toilet for guests, while 55 (11%) had no shower for guests. This situation might well be related to the small loans given to farmers, who as a result had little money to invest.

According to the survey, at the end of 1995 the average loan received by farmers was less than US$4,400, although the maximum ceiling was US$11,000 at that time. This is probably for two reasons. Firstly, program implementation was not well dispersed in the target area, and secondly, farmers felt reluctant to invest because of the low returns.

In this regard, it is recommended that the program should increase the size of loans for farmers, and give them to more farmers, so that government or cooperative loans can provide a greater share of farmers' investment.

Income

Unlike tourism farms, the income of the most farms inns is highly dependant on accommodation. According to the survey, 60% of the income of farm inns was generated from accommodation, 25% from selling farm products and 15% from serving food, although there was a wide range of variation between provinces. It is recommended that in future, farm inns take steps to diversify their income source. This could be done by selling farm produce, and also value added products such as processed special delicacies, traditional food items and local handicrafts. The potential is demonstrated by Chun-Nam Province, where 52% of income was from the sale of farm produce and 20% from cooked meals.

Poor Promotion

Farm inns and tourism farms are not widely advertised. Although the program is not the same as ordinary commercial tourism, it is necessary to advertise in order to attract visitors who live some distance away. The survey found that only some provinces distributed pamphlets during the tourism season (around 1,000 copies), with the expenses shared by the agricultural cooperatives, government agencies and farmers. Most villages with a farm inn used a cloth banner and signboard at the entrance of the village as the main form of advertisement. High standards of hospitality and service are necessary for a farm inn which wants to gain a good reputation.

It is recommended that local councils and agricultural cooperatives should improve their public relations and information activities in a systematic way, for example through increased use of electronic media.

Bibliography

- Becky Barrow (2010-01-22). "Cadbury's boss set to collect £12million pay-off while unions fear jobs bloodbath after Kraft takeover | Mail Online". London: Dailymail.co.uk. http://www.dailymail.co.uk/news/article-1244330/Cadburys-boss-set-collect-12million-pay-unions-fear-jobs-bloodbath-Kraft-takeover.html.

- Burn a Little Rubber, Melt a Lot of Hearts People Magazine July 23, 1990 "A teetotaler, Cruise footed the $13,000 bill-most of it for alcohol-for that New Year's Eve party in Charlotte (dubbed Cruisin' in the New Year) for 450 crew members and friends."

- C Michael Hall, Brock Cambourne, Liz Sharples, Niki Macionis, Wine Tourism Around the World: Development, Management and Markets, Elsevier 2000 ISBN 0-7506-4530-X

- David Remnick, "King of the World: Muhammad Ali and the Rise of an American Hero", Random House, 1998

- Elisabeth Hasselbeck tastes Redbridge, discusses celiac on The View. | National Foundation for Celiac Awareness

- Faulkner, Lord, Memoirs of a Statesman (posthumous autobiography)

- Gerard Butler Dot Net (2001-11-18). "Gerard Butler dot Net - Press Room - Latest News". Gerardbutler.net. http://www.gerardbutler.net/news/news_main.php?Action=Full&NewsID=341.

- Giddings, Edward Jonathan. American Christian Rulers, p. 66. New York: Bromfield & Company, 1890.
- Guy Adams. "Prince Andrew: the playboy prince" (2006-12-9), The Independent.
- Hester Lacey. "Focus: Alcohol - Danger that lurks on the alcoholic's 12 steps to" (2000-06-09), The Independent.
- Isaac Asimov (1991). Isaac Asimov's Treasury of Humor: A Lifetime Collection of Favorite Jokes, Anecdotes, and Limericks with Copious Notes on How to Tell Them and Why. Houghton Mifflin Books, 106. ISBN 0-395-57226-6.
- J Carlsen, S Charters, Edith Cowan University (editors), Global Wine Tourism, Cabi Publishing (2006)
- John, Patricia LaCaille (2008). Promoting Tourism in Rural America. National Agricultural Library, Rural Information Center. Retrieved December 30, 2008.
- Leibovich, Mark (September 16, 2008). "Riding the Rails With Amtrak Joe". The New York Times. http://thecaucus.blogs.nytimes.com/2008/09/16/riding-the-rails-with-amtrak-joe/.
- Lowe, Janet. "Damn Right!", p. 173. New York: John Wiley & Sons, Inc., 2000.
- Rookwood, Dan (4 July 2003). "My wife [Michelle Gayle doesn't drink at all. She's tea-total"]. The Guardian (London). http://www.guardian.co.uk/football/2003/jul/04/newsstory.sport3.
- Slate: "If you're a teetotaler, how come you know so much about booze?" Ken's response: His wife has been quizzing him with cocktail-themed flashcards.
- Vincent Gallo (Brown Bunny) - David Lamble / Claudesplace.com Interview
- Wilkerson, Chad (2003). "Travel and Tourism: An Overlooked Industry in the U.S. and Tenth District." Economic Review, Third Quarter 2003. Federal Reserve Board in Kansas. Retrieved December 30, 2008.

INDEX